To Kim —
Blessings to you !!!
"It's Really Good to See You"

Steven A. K.

IT'S REALLY GOOD TO
See You

STEVEN ANTHONY KING

Foreword by Les Brown

ISBN: 978-1-7367838-0-1 (paperback)
ISBN: 978-1-7367838-1-8 (eBook)

Cover Designed by TWA Solutions
Photo Credit: James Alexander

Disclaimer:
The information provided in this book is designed to provide helpful information on the subjects discussed. This book is not meant to be used, nor should it be used, to diagnose or treat any medical condition. For diagnosis or treatment of any medical problem, consult your own physician. The publisher and author are not responsible for any specific health or allergy needs that may require medical supervision and are not liable for any damages or negative consequences from any treatment, action, application or preparation, to any person reading or following the information in this book. References are provided for informational purposes only and do not constitute an endorsement of any websites or other sources. Readers should be aware that the websites listed in this book may change.

DEDICATION

To my mother, Elaine King.
Because of you, I am. I miss you. I love you. I honor you.

To Tina, my Proverbs 31 Wife.
Every day you prove to me that marrying you was one of the best decisions I ever made. This is your story as much as it is mine. You were my eyes when I could not see. We walked this journey together, hand-in-hand: the setbacks and the victories. It didn't break us, it made us stronger! If there is a way to love you more, I haven't found it yet, but I promise, I'll keep searching.

To my son, Kadeem, my daughters, Stephanee and Rachel, my granddaughter, the Princess Parker, and my family.
Thank you for being the reason I get up every day and strive to be the best that I can be. I love you all with everything that I am.

ACKNOWLEDGMENTS

Dr. Benjamin Freilich: Thank you for your care, concern, support, and persistence to make sure my sight was placed in the best hands (literally).

Dr. Stanley Chang: Thank you for never giving up and saving the quality of my life.

Michael King: Thank you for all of your prayers and support during this challenging period in my life. You are the best big brother I could ever have.

Smitty: My friend, my brother, my comrade. Words can't express my gratitude for our friendship.

Victoria Christopher Murray: My sensei! Thank you for being my coach, mentor, therapist, and the master architect of this book.

Yvette Hayward: Thank you for being the matchmaker that turned my dream into a reality.

Antrina Richardson: Thank you for your editing expertise.

ReShonda Tate Billingsly: Thank you for proofreading and your professional expertise.

Jessica Tilles: Thank you for designing the perfect book cover and formatting the interior. It embodies the true spirit of the book. Thank you for doing the final edits, as well. Your guidance has been a blessing.

James Alexander: Thank you for capturing the perfect picture for the book cover. Your photography skills are unmatched.

My 1199 Family: forty-six years and counting, we are so much more than friends. We are family, a village. When one of us wins we all win!!!

FOREWORD

You have something special; you have GREATNESS in you.

If you are familiar with my messages and career, you know I believe that greatness is an inherent trait that all of us possess. The unfortunate reality is that many of us never tap into our greatness, or even take the time to acknowledge what it means to be great.

We are essentially blind to the possibilities in our life because we take our gifts, talents, and abilities for granted.

The tragedy of life lies within what we take for granted, from the ability to think freely, dream big, and even—if you're sighted—the ability to simply use our eyes to see.

What would you do if you were suddenly faced with the possibility of losing your sight? Can you imagine how different the world would be for you? Would you grieve the impending loss, or would you use the situation as an opportunity to truly learn to live?

In *It's Really Good to See You*, Steven Anthony King shows us why we can't afford to treat "the little things" in life as insignificant. Steven shares the intimate details of his yearlong journey of almost losing his sight, and how he gained a deeper sense of love, giving, and compassion in the process. By leaning on his faith instead of fear, Steven was not only able to manifest his own healing, but he was also able to even help heal others in the process.

It's Really Good to See You has further opened my eyes to the beauty of the human spirit. I know that reading this book will do the same for you. Prepare to be guided through a riveting process of gaining physical, emotional, and spiritual wellness amid uncertainty.

If you're ready to tap into your greatness and need an example of faith, courage, and conviction, *It's Really Good to See You* is the book for you.

I am excited to see the success of Steven Anthony King. He's leaving his mark on the world and I know that your life will be enriched within these pages.

Yours in GREATNESS,

Les Brown
World's Leading Motivational
Speaker, and Bestselling Author

INTRODUCTION

May 31, 2017

I was still blind. I couldn't see anything other than people's feet because the gas bubble inserted into my eye to protect my retina had not yet dissolved. I had to keep my head down, but that wasn't going to stop me. I was going to attend this anniversary meeting because I had to be there for Fernando, who was my former sponsor in the twelve-step program I attend.

Fernando had left New York to live in Hawaii, and tonight he had returned to New York to celebrate his anniversary. It was because of our relationship that I had to be there.

Fernando had been one of my first sponsors, and now he was almost like an ambassador in the fellowship. He'd been clean for close to thirty years and because of his success, as well as the support he gave others, Fernando was absolutely beloved in New York. But no one in the fellowship loved and respected him more than me. He'd helped me so much in my recovery that no matter what, I wasn't going to miss this meeting, even if I couldn't see.

It had been fifteen days since I'd had the surgery. I'd just found out last month, in April, that I needed surgery, a Vitrectomy, to correct a hole in my macular. I was still in the healing process. Even though I'd had so many surgeries before, this was a process that was more complicated than anything I'd ever been through. But I was recovering, and that was my thought as I prepared to go see Fernando.

I was anxious about the meeting, though. So many emotions surged through me. When everyone saw me, would they judge me? Was I going to be bombarded with lots of questions? Would anyone there make a stupid comment as a joke that would hurt me?

These things were running through my mind, but alongside that, I was also excited. For the last few weeks, my life had been nothing more than home, hospitals, and the doctor's office. Tonight was a chance to bring some normalcy back into my life.

As we prepared to leave our apartment in New Jersey, more familiar feelings pushed aside the excitement. Every time I left the house, I felt helpless because my wife, Tina, had to help me do just about everything from the moment we stepped outside of the door. Once we were in the hallway, I was vulnerable because it was difficult to walk without my sight. Tina had to guide me through the hallway and down to the garage where we parked our car. Over these last couple of weeks of doctor visits, I tried to claim some independence. I'd memorized the number of steps I had to take down the hallway before we made a slight left turn to approach the door to the garage.

One thing I'd noticed since my surgery was how my senses had become more acute. As we walked down the hall,

I'd run my hands along the wall, searching for the familiar grooves where each wall panel met. Then, I could feel the slight changes of pressure in Tina's grip on my arm as we got closer to the garage.

With each trip out, I got better with the counting of steps and the feeling of the wall. But every time I had to walk with my wife beside me, I felt challenged by the thought that this could become the reality of my life, for the rest of my life. Although I felt those kinds of crushing feelings, I didn't show it. Even as I sometimes was on the edge of depression, I kept my chin up—though only figuratively—for my wife. Tina fed off my emotions and if she knew my dark thoughts, it would crush her.

I had to be emotionally strong for not only myself, but her as well. I had to do it because, even with my head down and the future of my sight uncertain, I was still the protector of the family, and protecting Tina was just what I did.

When we reached the garage, and once Tina opened the door, it was easy to tell that we were in an open space. Now, I had to be even more cautious because of the dips in the garage floor and the low-hanging pipes.

Once we were in the car, I could relax a bit, although I was still anxious. Now, the anxiety of how people would react to me returned. What would they think? What would they say when they saw me with my head down and being guided around by my wife?

However, while those questions were in my head, by the time Tina and I were inside and sitting in the meeting in Harlem, I felt empowered. This was something I needed to do, not only to support Fernando but to prove to myself that this latest challenge with my eyes wasn't beating me and that I didn't have to sit in the house and sulk, waiting to see if I was going to get better.

But then, those anxious thoughts I had in the car rushed back to me. There were people here I'd known for as long as nineteen years, but no matter how long, everyone in this room knew me as Big Steve. I'd worked out a lot, so Big Steve was my image. I was fit, my body was well-defined, and everything I did lived up to that name.

Now there was one part of my life that didn't live up to my name—my eyesight. I'd totally lost my vision in my right eye back in the '80s as the result of a surgery I'd had in Boston that just didn't work. I'd just had another surgery on my left eye and if that didn't work...

I'd inherited my severe near-sightedness from my mother. The medical term for what I'd lived with my entire life was high myopia. However, I had never mentioned it to too many people because how could I be Big Steve if I had such a weakness?

It wasn't so much that I was keeping my medical condition a secret, it just never came up in conversation. Over the last few months, I'd started opening up about my eye history with a few of my friends here. Tonight, though, everyone would see for themselves that I had a condition. Tonight, I was here without my ego, without my image. Everyone would see that I was still Big Steve, but I was a human being with imperfections. I just had to be prepared, and I felt ready. I'd given thought to what I would say and how I would explain what had been going on if anyone asked.

"I've had some challenges with my eyes," I would tell them. "All in all, I've had a total of eleven eye operations. I don't have sight in my right eye, and in my left eye, I have 20/20 vision to the tip of my nose. After that, it's a crapshoot."

That explanation would definitely break the ice, with them and for me. From there, I'd share my whole story if anyone wanted to know. I was ready to talk honestly to the men and women who'd supported me over the years.

The only thing is, if anyone wanted to talk to me, I'd have to answer them with my head down the entire time.

CHAPTER 1

I was seven years old the first time I had to lay on an operating table. That would be the beginning, the first of fourteen eye operations.

Just a few months before that first operation, I'd begun to notice something that looked and felt like a purple cloud from the side of my eye. Actually, it was more like a purple curtain that was billowing in a gentle breeze. It was annoying, especially since as time passed the cloud began to eclipse more of my eye.

It became so prevalent that I mentioned it to my mother. Right away she took me to Dr. Vogel, her doctor. I later learned that Dr. Vogel was a retinal specialist who told my mother that a tear in my retina was causing fluid to leak into my eye. That diagnosis led me to my first operation and a week's stay in the children's ward of Montefiore Medical Center.

Since that time, I'd had ten operations, no vision in my right eye, and a scleral buckle in my left one that kept that retina in place. After having gone through so much, I definitely knew something was going on with my eye and in January 2017, I noticed something different. Something I'd never experienced started happening. It was just a little shift in my vision. It wasn't the normal purple curtain, which I called the ominous curtain of doom that affected my peripheral vision for all of those years. This time, the challenge was in the center of my eye.

I did nothing about it at first. I thought maybe it was just floaters, which were little squiggly shadows floating around inside my eye. The floaters were nothing more than debris from scar tissue that had built up from all of my surgeries. Sometimes, I thought of my eye like a fish tank with all kinds of floating algae. Other times, I compared it to an old school discotheque—with floaters and flashing lights; there was always something going on in my eye.

This time, though, whatever was happening was unfamiliar, and I hoped it would just go away. Looking back, I was in a state of denial, ignoring that 'oh no, not again' feeling inside of me. So, for weeks, I figuratively covered my eyes and told myself that nothing was really wrong.

But as the symptoms persisted through January and February, I couldn't ignore them any longer; whatever was going on wasn't going away.

It was the beginning of March when I finally called the doctor I trusted most over the years. Dr. Topilow had operated on me three out of the ten surgeries I'd had, beginning when I was sixteen. To this day, I give him all the credit for saving my vision. (I called my left eye "his eye" since he'd saved it.) By saving that eye, he'd saved the quality of my life as well.

Over the years, we'd lost touch, then reconnected when I was forty-three years old. But this time, when I dialed his number, it was disconnected. When I first heard the automated message, I thought I'd dialed wrong. So, I hung up and dialed again. When I heard the message the second time, I knew it wasn't a mistake.

Now, I was a bit alarmed. That was weird for a doctor's number to be disconnected without a forwarding number or someone there to answer and give some information.

I didn't want to panic, but I had to find Dr. Topilow. He was the only one I wanted to work with in this situation. Not only did he know my history and all of my complications, but he still remembered me. He'd proven that when we reconnected years earlier...

Since I'd last seen Dr. Topilow, there had been so many changes in my vision, though nothing was too serious. It was just the natural progression of aging, but I'd wanted to check in with Dr. Topilow.

As I sat in his office that day, with classical music playing in the background, I watched Dr. Topilow, thinking that he was always so sharp in the way he dressed. On that day, he wore a cashmere sweater vest over a pinstriped shirt with cuff links and a bow tie. But it wasn't just the way he dressed that I admired. I watched him as he glanced over my charts that he'd kept for almost thirty years.

As I sat there, he recited everything about my case, as if three decades hadn't passed...

When I'd visited him that day, he'd spoken to me as if I were his peer, although he still addressed me by the name he called me when I was sixteen— Kiddo.

So when I heard that recording, stating the number had been disconnected, I was at a point of desperation. I felt kind of like a kid who'd gotten himself into a situation, and all he needed to get out of it was his dad. That's what Dr. Topilow meant to me; I just wanted my doctor.

The hunt for Dr. Topilow continued for days and as I searched for him, Tina and I kept having the same conversation.

"Something's wrong," was what I'd said to my wife just about every day. "Doctors don't just disappear; their numbers just don't go out of service. That doesn't happen."

"I know," Tina agreed.

"Especially not with someone like Doctor Topilow," I added.

In the middle of what was probably our fourth or fifth conversation about Dr. Topilow, Tina said something she hadn't said before. "Why don't you look his name up in the obituaries."

All the days we'd been talking about this and that thought had never occurred to me. It seemed to come out of nowhere from Tina and it hit me like two or three tons of bricks. But it also made sense; that would explain how the doctor had just disappeared.

"I'll look it up," my wife said.

It took Tina just a few minutes to search for his name on her phone, and her hunch had been right. Dr. Topilow had just passed away in January of that year, at the relatively young age of sixty-six.

I was beyond sad, I was panic-stricken. I didn't have my doctor. The one guy, who'd saved my quality of life and thereby had saved me, couldn't do it again.

Dr. Topilow was gone.

I was devastated, and I was depressed, but I couldn't stay in that place. There was something wrong with my eye, and if I didn't do something about it, it could get worse. The first step I had to take was finding another doctor. It wasn't going to be easy because I couldn't have just anyone working on my eye.

After thinking about it, I reached out to Tracy, a young man from the fellowship who I'd sponsored since the 2000s. It was then that Tracy revealed to me he had vision challenges and we shared similar visual conditions. At one point, I wore prescription glasses and contact lenses to improve my vision, and Tracy had done the same thing. While our conditions were similar, the state of our eyes was different. Tracy still had his vision in both eyes.

When we discovered we shared more than our recovery journey, we were shocked. "I never thought I'd meet anyone who could identify with what I'd gone through visually," Tracy had told me back then.

I agreed with him. After he told me his story and I shared mine, I knew it was God who had brought Tracy and me together. Now, years later, I needed him in a different way.

As soon as I called Tracy and explained what was going on, he referred me to his doctor, Dr. Chess. "He'll be good, Steve," Tracy told me. "He's very thorough and I like him."

I didn't want too much time to pass, so within the week, I was on my way to see Dr. Chess. I'd taken off early from work, wanting to give myself and the doctor as much time as needed, but the moment I walked into the office on 86th Street, I got a bad vibe.

The waiting room was filled with elderly people. When I stepped inside, I felt an undertone in the atmosphere; the place was not as professional as the offices I'd visited over the years.

But even though I didn't have the best of feelings, I stayed because Tracy had such a good experience. Stepping up to the receptionist, I gave my name and was told to have a seat among the others in the full waiting room.

I didn't have to wait too long before a forty-something-year-old Hispanic man called me into the back. When he greeted me, I felt a bit better. He was friendly and professional. It was obvious in the way he carried himself, the way he dressed (in a shirt and tie beneath his lab coat), and the way he put me at ease. He took pride in not only his job but his appearance, too. That said a lot to me.

After I explained my situation to the technician, he said, "Okay, let's see what we have going on here. We're going to run a couple of tests."

No matter what doctor I visited, the tests were always the same. First, it was a vision exam, which had come a long way from the charts that doctors had on the wall decades ago. Now, with the lights turned out, the letters were projected on the wall.

Right after he turned out the lights, the technician offered me a black spoon. "Use this to cover your right eye," he told me.

I shook my head and told him what I told every technician, "I won't need that. My right eye is a prosthetic."

After the vision test, I sat in a chair, and in front of me was a machine that looked like the coin-operated viewers seen on observation decks. The machine was to check the surface of my eye, the cornea. Then finally, I sat at the OCP, another machine that scanned a digital picture of the back of my eye. These high-tech machines weren't available in the early years when I began this journey.

Once he finished, the technician studied my results. "I see what the problem is; I see what's going on."

"What is it?"

He shook his head. "The doctor will talk to you about it."

"Is it something that can be fixed?" I pressed, wanting an answer now, especially since he'd said he had the information that I needed to know.

"Yeah, of course," he said casually, putting me a bit at ease once again. "The doctor will talk to you," he repeated, letting me know he wasn't able to say anything more. He didn't want to give me false hope, nor let me down. "The doctor will be right with you."

So, I sat in the office and waited for Dr. Chess, not wanting to imagine the worst, wanting to stay hopeful for the best news. I'd sat in these rooms, waiting for doctors over the years. It was never for longer than five minutes.

A few minutes later, the door opened and a female Russian doctor walked inside. After she introduced herself, she asked, "What brings you here today?"

Wait a minute, this isn't Dr. Chess, I thought as she examined me. After about five minutes, I asked her where was the doctor I expected to see.

My question seemed to surprise her a bit, and she answered abruptly, "Well, you will be fine," which didn't answer my question at all.

So, I repeated, "Where is Dr. Chess? I have an appointment with him."

"I will examine you," she told me again, her words rushed, as if I was bothering her with my questions.

Now I was past annoyed; I was getting to the point of being pissed. What was going on here? Was I in the middle of some kind of bait and switch scheme? I'd had enough experience with enough doctors to know this was not the way things were done. So what were they doing in this office? What kind of game were they running?

I pressed, pushing back, letting her know I wanted to see Dr. Chess. But she pushed back, too, not backing down. The way she responded to me, I could tell she was used to telling people what to do and people would just accept what she said. But I was not one of the elderly people in the waiting room. So, I kept pushing, I kept pressing and finally, when she stepped out of the room, all I could do was hope that she went in search of Dr. Chess.

Within five minutes, the door opened again, and this time a short, stocky, bald guy, who reminded me a little of George Costanza from Seinfeld, entered. He wasn't goofy like the TV character; Dr. Chess definitely had doctor swag. If George had an older, more professional brother, Dr. Chess would have been him.

"I'm Dr. Chess. I'm sorry for the confusion."

"I appreciate that. My friend recommended you and spoke so highly of you that you were the doctor I wanted to see."

When he nodded, I left it there, wanting to keep the peace. There was no need to take this fight any further now that Dr. Chess was in front of me. I just wanted to get down to the business of my eye.

Dr. Chess started with, "So, tell me about your history."

I ran it all down to him, starting with, "I'm blind in one eye and I've had ten operations."

He didn't say, "Wow," but I saw his surprise.

His reaction did not surprise me. Even though this was his business, the number of operations I'd had was staggering. Definitely, something that wasn't common.

"Okay, well, let me take a look into your eye."

This was one final exam that all these doctors performed. Laying back on the examination table, with the paper crinkled beneath my weight, took me back to the first time I had to lay this way. I was just seven years old, and I was so scared, not understanding at all what was going on...

April 1972

The cloud in my eye had just started, but as soon as I told my mother, she brought me right here to this doctor. He seemed nice enough for an older guy. But then, he asked me to lie down on an examination table.

I hopped onto the table; the paper crinkled when I sat on it.

"Now lay back," Dr. Vogel told me.

I did as he said and wondered why there was another table with a sketching pad on it right next to where I lay.

Once I was on my back, Dr. Vogel said, "I'm going to use this drop to dilate your eye, okay?"

It sounded like he was asking my permission, but he didn't wait for me to agree. He put the drops in, told me to close my eyes and keep them closed. Then, about twenty minutes later, when I opened my eyes, Dr. Vogel stood above me with some kind of contraption strapped onto his forehead. That was strange enough until he clicked a switch on the side and a bright light shined right

15

into my eyes. I would later compare what Dr. Vogel wore to a coal miner's headlamp.

I squinted against the brightness and with that light shining in my eyes, Dr. Vogel picked up a magnifying glass.

"Okay, Steven, now I'm going to look in your eye." With his fingers, he spread my eye wide. "I'm looking in the back of your eye to see what's wrong," he said, explaining what he was doing.

But I was hardly listening to him because of the way I felt. What he was doing didn't hurt physically, but that bright light—I wanted to get away from it. With the way the doctor held my eye open, I couldn't even blink for relief. My body tensed with the discomfort.

As he looked into my eye, I figured out why there was a sketch pad on the table next to where I was laying. Dr. Vogel was sketching what he saw. I learned much later that he was working from a stencil of the eyeball that had all the major parts of the retina on it.

"Relax," the doctor kept telling me.

Relax? How was I supposed to do that with the light and the magnifying glass (that made the light more intense) and his fingers propping my eye open?

Then, he said, "Look down."

For some reason, I thought he would let me go so I could look down, but he still held my eye. I tried to look down and squint at the same time, just to get a little bit of relief from the bright light.

"Look left."

I did as the doctor told me, though now I couldn't see anything. The light had blinded me.

"Look right."

Now it was excruciating. This torture made my eye water, and a tear seeped from the corner before it trickled down the side of my face. I could see nothing, except for the blinding whiteness of the light.

Finally, after what felt like an eternity, but was probably only thirty minutes, the doctor released me from the torture and clicked off the light.

Dr. Chess was now doing the same thing. He clicked off the light from his headgear and for a few moments, all I could see was the doctor's silhouette before my vision slowly returned.

As I adjusted to the normal light, Dr. Chess studied the sketch he'd drawn and the image that had been taken earlier. After comparing the two, he said, "I see it. You have a macular hole."

Out of all the doctors I'd seen and all the operations I'd had, I had never heard that term before.

"Is that the same as a detached retina?" I asked because that was the familiar term to me.

"No. This is more like a pothole in the middle of the retina. That's what's causing the squiggles in the center of your vision."

"How does this happen?"

"Well, with your visual history, the fragile nature of your retina, and all the trauma your retina has received, this isn't uncommon." He paused. "It can be fixed. There is a surgical procedure that will repair this for you."

I breathed with a bit of relief. I wasn't excited about another surgery, but if that was what I needed, at least this doctor was giving me the solution. My relief, however, didn't last for long.

Dr. Chess took all my hope away when he added, "However, I wouldn't do the surgery. I wouldn't touch your eye with a ten-foot pole. Your eye is a land mine."

His words were shocking and, at first, I sat there thinking about all I'd been through, which made what he said understandable. Just in this eye alone, I'd had four retinal detachment repairs along with a cataract removal. Like I said before, a lot was going on, but I'd come so far. To hear a doctor now telling me that there was help, but he couldn't be the one to help me, made me feel helpless.

It must have been my look of despair that made him say, "I'm so sorry." He then repeated, "But like I said, your eye is a land mine. I noticed that you have a scleral buckle."

"Yes, Dr. Harvey Topilow did that."

His eyes lit up when I said that. "Yes, I knew him. What he did in your eye was really a masterpiece of medical work."

That's what every doctor told me about Dr. Topilow, who had attached my retina onto a scleral buckle to keep it stable.

"Dr. Topilow was certainly the best in the field," he told me. "He will be greatly missed."

"I just found out that he passed away," I said, feeling a bit emotional about saying that. "That's why I came to you."

His eyes were sad, as if he was sorry. But still, he said, "I've been in the business for forty years, I do surgeries all the time. I could do the surgery you need—one, two, three, but like I said, it's too fragile a situation."

Even though he wouldn't agree to do the surgery, I still had a few questions since he'd diagnosed my condition: Would my eye get progressively worse? What was the worst-case scenario for me? Would I go blind from this?

He answered my questions patiently. "You won't go blind," Dr. Chess assured me, "but you will lose all the vision in the center of your eye so the quality of your sight will definitely diminish."

Losing vision in the center of my eye wasn't an option, especially since I had already lost some peripheral vision from all the scar tissue that had built up from prior surgeries. So if I lost my center vision, I would damn near be blind.

"Will I be able to get around?"

"Yes, you will. You'll be able to get around, but you won't be able to read and it will be difficult to watch television. You definitely won't be able to drive."

The truth was harsh, but his tone was not. I could tell that Dr. Chess felt for me; he was trying to be as compassionate as possible, but also as direct as he could be, too. He wasn't going to sugarcoat it; he didn't want to give me false hope.

Even though it was hard to hear, I was grateful for the education. At least now I could focus on the next steps. Since Dr. Chess wouldn't be able to help me, I started focusing on getting a second opinion.

"Thank you," I told Dr. Chess as I stood and shook his hand. There was nothing more that I needed (or wanted) to hear from him.

He nodded. "You know what? I'm going to recommend a company that specializes in visual aids that will help you with reading and tasks like that."

After he gave me the card, I shook his hand once again. I believed he was telling me what he thought was best and there was nothing I could be except grateful.

My mind was racing as I walked out of that office. All kinds of negative thoughts started to creep in. After ten years

19

of a wonderful marriage, I am now going to be a burden on my wife and Tina will surely leave me. I won't be able to provide for my family, my son and two daughters, who are grown and who can take care of themselves, but still, I can't be there if they need me...I won't be able to see my granddaughter grow up.

Images played through my mind: I saw myself walking down the street with a silver metal cane, but then, that scene switched to my holding onto the leash of a seeing-eye dog. I imagined how hard it was going to be to handle people's reactions to me as a blind man.

Suddenly, I caught myself. There was no room for any of this negativity. I had to draw on all the spiritual strength that I'd sought and was within me. I had to rely on my faith and my trust in God.

So now, with those negative thoughts pushed aside and more positive thoughts in my mind, I only had one question: What would I do next?

CHAPTER 2

The next day when I returned to my office, I was in a sullen mood. I was no longer at the point of hysteria, thinking that I was going to be blind. No, because of my faith I was staying far away from that thought. But I was in the shit-I'm-going-to-have-another-operation mode and because I was feeling down, I went to talk to one of the partners of the company where I worked.

It wasn't that Alex and I were really good friends, although I did consider him and me to be closer than normal colleagues. I wanted to keep him in the loop regarding what was going on with me—and I went to him because I was looking for some…I'm not sure of the right word—maybe it was comfort.

When I knocked on Alex's door, he invited me in. I sat down, ready to have a serious discussion about what was going on.

"Alex, I'm facing a serious situation with my eyesight."

Alex looked up from his computer, now giving me his full attention. However, when I finished, his response wasn't at all what I expected.

"Look, Steve," he began, "you just need to accept it. It is what it is. Just begin to adjust to not being able to see."

I wasn't angry by what he said, but I certainly was shocked. I just stared at him; knowing Alex, though, I knew he wasn't pushing me aside. He had no malicious intent at all. He wanted to hear my story and I think he was sure he was giving me good advice. To him, he was just helping me to learn to accept what he thought couldn't be changed, he was trying to get me to man up. That was his pep talk to me because I think he was incapable of anything else; he was incapable of empathizing with what I was going through.

It was a weird encounter because he was trying to get me to accept something that I was never going to accept. I wasn't about to give in to this. I wasn't going to crawl into a corner and die. I was going to fight because the only thing in the world that would be worse than being blind, was becoming blind and wondering: What if…what if I'd done this? What if I'd done that? What if I'd done just a little bit more to find another doctor who could help me?

I was never going to live a life of what-ifs and regrets. I was not giving up in any kind of way. All I had to do was figure out how to find the right doctor. How could I find that doctor who'd be willing to operate on my eye, the land mine?

I didn't know how I was going to do it, but I would. I'd find a doctor who would help me. In the meantime, though, I'd have to give my new doctor everything he needed to be successful because I had so much going on. He'd need my medical records. Somehow, I had to find out what happened to my records from Dr. Topilow.

I began a hunt for my records, but as the days passed, so did my optimism and my hope started to wane. Even with all of that positivity inside of me, a bit of negativity seeped in. Some of it was because I hadn't yet been able to find my medical records from Dr. Topilow. But the other part of it was that my mind began to fill with images of what would happen if I couldn't find a doctor to operate on me. What would happen if Dr. Chess' predictions came true?

Already I was affecting the plans Tina and I had. We were in the middle of planning a trip for our tenth wedding anniversary in May. This would be our second time going to Aruba for the Soul Beach Music Fest. We already had everything booked, but knowing that I needed surgery, a celebration in Aruba didn't seem likely.

Even though I was really disappointed, I refused to allow this situation to drag me down into a dark abyss. I continued doing what I knew how to do: I prayed, I meditated, and I consciously affirmed that my sight was going to be okay.

I kept talking to God and then my perseverance paid off. One of the doctors in the medical building where Dr. Topilow had his office directed me to the owner of the building, who was an eye doctor himself and knew Dr. Topilow.

"It was a terrible loss," he said to me after I told him who I was and what I needed.

"Yes, Dr. Topilow had been working with me for years," I told him. "That's why I'm trying to find my medical records."

"Oh, well then you should check with Dr. Freilich because when Topilow retired, he began directing his patients to Dr. Freilich."

My hope was rejuvenated when he gave me Dr. Freilich's contact information. I made an appointment to see the doctor right away.

CHAPTER 3

It was a rainy, dreary day when I traveled in the late afternoon to Englewood, New Jersey, but the weather didn't match my mood. My hope was back up as my prayers continued; I felt God with me.

Dr. Freilich's office was in a small office building in something that was like a suburban commercial complex. When I stepped inside the office, right away I felt better than when I'd walked into Dr. Chess' office. In the corner, a television hung high and the evening news was coming on as I signed in with the receptionist. Just a few minutes later, I was taken back to see Dr. Freilich.

The moment he walked into the office, I thought he looked just like a doctor: he was five feet eight inches tops, balding with a beard, and much younger than Dr. Topilow. I would later learn that Dr. Freilich's father and Dr. Topilow were close colleagues.

I sat in the chair in the small examination room while Dr. Freilich rested on a stool with wheels.

"So tell me, what's going on with you?" Dr. Freilich's tone was serious, just like all the other doctors I'd met.

I told him I'd come to him because I thought he might have my medical records, but that I also needed help. Like I always did, I gave him my medical bio; all the surgeries I'd had, how there was no vision in my right eye, and how Dr. Topilow had operated on my left eye three times when I was sixteen.

Just like when I was with Dr. Chess, it was a bit emotional to talk about Dr. Topilow as I thought back to all he'd done for me. As I spoke, I saw the genuine sympathy in Dr. Freilich's eyes and all I hoped was that he would be able to help. I prayed that he'd be willing to do the surgery since Dr. Topilow had referred all of his clients to him. If Dr. Topilow trusted him, then so did I.

He had me lay back on the table and, once again, I had to bear the bright light in my eye. Right away, he noticed the scleral buckle.

"Dr. Topilow put the buckle in your eye?"

When I told him he had, Dr. Freilich said the same words as every other doctor—he called it a masterpiece.

"Well, the doctors you've seen are right," he said after his examination was over. He sat on the stool and rolled closer to the chair where I was sitting. "You have a macular hole in your eye."

I waited for Dr. Freilich to tell me whether he was willing to do the surgery. "I can't do the surgery," he said. Then, he added, "But I can put you in touch with a doctor who specializes in this type of procedure."

For a moment, I leaned back a bit. What was he saying? That he didn't want to even consider touching my eye? He was already referring me to someone else?

25

"The doctor I'm talking about studied under Stanley Chang and Chang is the best guy in the world for this kind of procedure. This doctor used to be Stanley Chang's partner."

The way he talked about Stanley Chang made me ask, "Well, why do we have to stop at the partner? Can you get me in touch with Dr. Chang?"

I think my question surprised him for a moment, but not for long because he nodded. "I can definitely reach out to Dr. Chang and see what happens."

Now, I was expecting Dr. Freilich to tell me to give him a couple of days to track down Stanley Chang. However, right then, as I sat in the room, he pulled out his cell phone and my eyes widened with surprise. Was he going to call Dr. Stanley Chang right now? No doctor would do that, but even as I had that thought, I listened as he made the call.

From his side of the conversation, I could tell he'd reached the receptionist and Dr. Chang wasn't available. But instead of just leaving a message, Dr. Freilich said, "Well, can you get ahold of him? Let him know it's Dr. Freilich. I have a special patient that I need him to see immediately."

Whoa! I couldn't believe how hard this doctor was going for me, even though we'd just met. The receptionist seemed to be putting up a blockade, but it was clear Dr. Freilich wasn't going to be denied.

I understood what was going on. Dr. Freilich had just told me that Dr. Chang was the best in the world. Everyone was probably trying to get in touch with him. To get on his schedule had to be something like trying to get a table at an exclusive restaurant…where there was a waiting list that was surely at least six months long.

If that was the case, that didn't seem to matter to Dr. Freilich. He told the receptionist, "Just have him call me back as soon as he finishes with his patient. I'll give you my cell phone number."

That was another whoa moment for me. He was making it clear that this was urgent.

After he gave her his number, he reiterated, "Please, make sure that he calls me as soon as he gets out." Then he hung up and said to me, "Okay, well, you heard me. I left a message; I'm going to make sure that I speak with him today. If he doesn't get back to me in the next hour, I'll call him back. So, I'll contact you as soon as I hear from him."

"Okay," I said and thanked the doctor profusely. He didn't have to do all of this, and I wanted him to know that I was grateful.

When I walked outside, I hadn't felt that good in a long time. Dr. Freilich had left me with so much optimism, with so much hope. I knew he would do everything he could to reach Dr. Chang.

Later that evening, when I was settled at home with Tina, my cell phone rang. The 201 area code meant it was from New Jersey. When I answered, it was Dr. Freilich.

"Listen, Steven. I spoke with Dr. Chang and he's able to see you next Monday."

Monday? Today was Tuesday. That meant that Dr. Freilich had set me up to see the top doctor in the world for my situation in less than a week. What were the chances of this? I bet I'd have a better chance of winning the lottery.

I thanked Dr. Freilich over and over again.

"You don't have to thank me, but you're welcome. Make sure you stay in touch with me. I called you from my cell phone, so keep my number and call me if you have any questions. Let me know after you speak to Dr. Chang."

Again, I couldn't stop thanking him and when I hung up, all I could do was sit back and meditate for a moment. It looked like all the prayers and all the meditation and all of my talks with God were being answered. He was guiding me, directing me, and making something that seemed impossible happen.

My sight was going to be fine, just like I'd been affirming. God had guaranteed it. He'd put me in touch with the best in the world and now, I would see Stanley Chang in less than a week.

CHAPTER 4

It was Monday and the first of May. A new week, a new month, a new beginning. That was the hope I had as I walked into Dr. Chang's 53rd Street office in Manhattan, once again knowing God was with me.

It had only been six days since I'd seen Dr. Freilich and one thing I could say—New Jersey doctors and their environments were so different than city doctors. Dr. Chang was part of the Columbia University ophthalmology department. His office was in a fancy high-rise, but what was weird was the moment I walked into Dr. Chang's office, I felt as if I'd been there before. It wasn't a déjà vu moment, it wasn't a feeling—I had been in this office before; I just couldn't remember when or why. That wasn't unusual, though. My memory bank was overloaded with the number of appointments and the number of doctors I'd seen over the years.

After checking in with the receptionist, I was almost immediately taken to the back by the assistant, a young woman this time.

"Okay, first I'm going to check your vision," she said. I was sitting in the familiar examination chair that all eye doctors had.

When she handed me that black plastic spoon to cover my right eye, I shook my head and told her what I told every doctor, "I won't be needing that."

After the vision test, I sat back in the chair. She placed a few drops in my eye and continued the preliminary tests. I wondered how many drops had been put into my eyes over the years. How many tissues had I been given to wipe my eyes? The sights, the sounds, the smells of being in this office were all so familiar.

After she asked me about my symptoms, she took me into a room to take a scan of my eye—another standard procedure. A few minutes later, we were back in the examination room.

"Okay, Dr. Chang will be with you in a moment," she said.

I sat, waiting, knowing that it wouldn't be more than five minutes. But five minutes is a long time to be sitting in a room alone, thinking about your future—when your sight was in jeopardy.

Today I was filled with so many more feelings than usual. I was about to be in front of the preeminent ophthalmologist who could handle my condition. I was filled with a bit of curiosity—who was this man, the one considered to be one of the best in the world? Then, I had some skepticism—was he really as good as everyone said? Finally, it was hard not to feel anxious. Suppose Dr. Chang took one look at me and made the decision that Dr. Chess and Dr. Freilich had made...that he couldn't do it. Where would I be if the best in the world turned me down?

As I sat there with all of those thoughts going through my mind, what I had most was hope. Even though I wasn't excited about another surgery, at least there was a surgery that could fix my condition and save my quality of life. I had to remind myself to stay grateful for that and for the fact that I was even sitting in this office.

That thought made me smile a little. Over the last few days, I'd built Dr. Chang up to be almost a mythical character and now, I wondered what he'd look like, what would he act like?

Just as I had those thoughts, the door opened and Dr. Chang walked into the room. He was taller than I expected and he seemed to be a man who was in fairly good shape, especially for an older man, maybe in his sixties. One of the first things I noticed was that he didn't wear glasses, and inside, that made me chuckle.

"Hello," he said. His presence filled the room as he introduced himself, though of course, he needed no introduction. "And you're Steven King."

"Yes," I said.

He asked me a little about myself and I told him that Harvey Topilow had been my doctor.

"Yes, Harvey passed. That's a shame, he was a good man. We were good friends. We studied together at Columbia University way back, a long time ago." He chuckled a little. "In the seventies."

Hearing that he'd been friends with Dr. Topilow lifted my confidence in this man even more. I went on to tell him the story of how I'd met Dr. Topilow when I was only sixteen years old. Dr. Chang listened intently and after I'd told the

31

whole story, he said, "Harvey must have been just starting out back then."

I nodded. "Yes, I think he was in his late twenties, maybe early thirties."

"Okay, let me check out your eyes."

He pressed the button in the chair where I was sitting and it slowly began to recline. As I lay beneath the light, I tried to calm my thoughts, though it was hard. My mind once again took me back over the decades of my journey, but I kept my focus on the future. My prayer was that this would be fixed.

When Dr. Chang clicked off the light, he waited for me to sit up before he told me the same thing that Dr. Chess and Dr. Freilich had said, "You have a macular hole." But unlike the other doctors, he added, "And I can do the surgery."

Those words filled me with the greatest relief.

Then he gave me what I called the doctor's non-guarantee. "There's a seventy-five percent chance that we can fix this," he said. "But there could be some complications."

"Okay." I nodded. "I understand. So, what are the risks?"

"Well, there's a risk that the retina could detach and there could be hemorrhaging of the eye," he said, giving it to me straight. He then gave me the bottom line. "I can do the surgery, and while there are no guarantees, I think this will be good for you."

With his words, I was able to breathe more deeply, think more clearly. "What about insurance?" I asked.

Dr. Chang wasn't sure about what would be covered and what wouldn't be, but he didn't seem concerned about that, even though I was. These surgeries were expensive. But he changed the subject to what he could do.

"This is one of my specialties. In fact, there's only one more person in the world who's done more of these surgeries than me. A doctor in Spain."

"Oh," I said, a bit surprised since I hadn't heard of anyone else.

There was so much for me to process and I took a few moments, trying to think if I had any other questions. However, Dr. Chang interpreted my silence for something else.

He said, "If you want, I can put you in touch with the doctor in Spain, but there will be complications."

It sounded like he thought I was questioning his skill, which I was not doing at all.

He continued. "If you go with that doctor, you will have to stay in Spain for your recovery." He went on to explain more about the surgery and the healing process.

"Once the surgery is over, you still won't be healed," Dr. Chang began. "The surgery repairs the hole, but this retina is still very vulnerable to re-detaching. So a gas bubble is inserted beneath the retina." From there he explained that the bubble would help support the retina as it healed from the surgery. "But for the bubble to do its job, you're going to have to do your job. You'll have to keep your head down, in a certain position, for the whole time you're healing, or your eye will never heal."

"How long will I have to do that?" I asked.

"You'll have to keep your head in a face-down position for about two weeks. That's why if you want to have this done in Spain, you'll have to recover over there. For a minimum of two to three months."

"That long?"

He nodded. "Even when you're asleep, you'll have to sleep in a certain position. There are chairs and pillows that will help you do this," he said. "The success of the surgery is contingent upon this."

I couldn't imagine walking around and holding my head down like that for two straight weeks. Already that felt like a lot of pressure, knowing that holding my head like that was part of the surgery's success. In a way, I felt like I was responsible for my own healing.

But what other choice did I have? I had to make this work; it wasn't like I had a spare eye in the trunk. I only had vision in one eye, and holding my head down seemed like a small price to pay to maintain that vision.

This was a lot for me to absorb while sitting in the doctor's office. I couldn't wait to have the chance to go home, talk this over with Tina, and think about it.

But Dr. Chang had other plans. "So, if you want me to do this, we can do the surgery on the ninth."

"The ninth?" I repeated, surprised that he was already talking about scheduling the operation. "Of this month?"

"Yes, next week."

Wow! I'd come here to meet Dr. Chang and to see if he would even consider my case. Now, we were already talking about actually doing the surgery. This was moving so fast; suddenly, it was very real.

"I'd want to get my hands on your records," Dr. Chang said. "It would really be good if I had them."

"I'm working on that," I said. "I thought another doctor had them, but I'm going to still try to find them." Even though I said that, my thoughts were beyond his concern about my records. I was still thinking about the surgery that he wanted to do next week.

I understood that Dr. Chang being at the top of his field didn't spend a lot of time with patients, and he certainly didn't have a lot of time to spend with someone who wasn't sure what he wanted to do when he had so many patients who would be happy to be in my position.

However, this felt rushed. There was no way I wanted to make such a serious decision so quickly. Especially because I still had to find out about the insurance and what this would mean for me financially.

When I brought this up again, Dr. Chang said, "Listen, the insurance is the least of your worries. We can always work something out." He brought me back to the reality that the number one concern had to be taking care of my eye.

I didn't want to sound as if I wasn't sure, but I had to ask, "If I don't have the surgery, what's the worst-case scenario?"

"You won't be completely blind, but you won't have a good quality of life."

That was exactly what Dr. Chess had told me. "Okay," I said, knowing he had other patients to see. I thanked him for his time, told him I wanted to think about it, but would get back to him, and then I left.

I was in a bit of a daze. I'd walked into his office with skepticism, curiosity, and anxiety, but I was leaving with only anxiety. It was all real now. The hunt for finding the person who could help me was over. I'd just sat in front of him and he'd answered all my questions.

There was nothing else left to do except make the decision. The rubber had just truly met the road.

CHAPTER 5

I had to weigh all the options. I had to count all the costs, not only on the financial side, but I had to take the entire surgery and everything that came with it into consideration.

This was a heavy decision, and I wanted to talk it through. There were people in my life who helped me with that, one being my brother, Michael.

I am the youngest of three siblings. I have a sister, Deborah, who's ten years older, and my brother, Michael, eight years older. Growing up, Michael and I spent little time together because of the difference in our ages, but all of that changed as adults, especially whenever I had to talk through something serious. Michael stepped up, giving me that big brother support, protection, and spiritual comfort I truly needed.

My brother is a Muslim now, and although I don't practice Islam, I believe he believes he has a strong spiritual connection to his Higher Power; I've seen evidence of that in his life.

I told him what Dr. Chang had discussed with me and Michael just listened, allowing me to talk it out; he encouraged me and told me he knew whatever I decided, it would be right for me.

Next, I reached out to Smitty. He was part of a group of men from the fellowship that I called the Council of Elders, though that was not their official name. These men were just more experienced members who were always in the meetings, but they were full of wisdom—wise men in the village.

Smitty had already played a very important role in my life. My father passed away before I was five years old, so there was not much I remembered about him. For so much of my life, I searched for a father figure and when I was fifty, Smitty stepped up at a time when I really needed that.

Smitty, with his soft-spoken voice and calm demeanor, carried an aura of serenity. Whenever he spoke, he had a peaceful tone, peaceful energy. No matter what I would be going through, he always calmed me down, leaving me with a sense of peace.

About a year before, Smitty and I had really connected when he shared at a meeting that he was having trouble with his eyes. Any time someone shared anything about their vision, I sat up straight in my chair and zoomed in on their words.

Smitty and I had been coming to this particular meeting for years, but after he shared that, I met him outside of the room and told him I had some visual challenges, too.

"I can really identify with your struggle," I said after I told him a little bit about what I'd been through with my eyesight.

"Thank you. I appreciate you saying that," Smitty said.

"I'm going to call you," I told him. "And maybe I can help walk you through this."

From that point, we became close. He was not only struggling with his vision, but he was battling other health issues as well. We became each other's support system that year, and he helped me take the focus away from my own challenges.

So, of course, Smitty would be one who I would call now, and like my brother, he listened, got excited with the prospect that Dr. Chang could help me, and left me with a feeling like I could handle this.

Next, I called Dr. Freilich as I'd promised. He was happy that Dr. Chang agreed to take my case, and once again, he reiterated that I would have the best doctor in the world taking care of me. When I told him I needed time to think about it, Dr. Freilich understood.

"Just know you will be in the best hands," he said. "And remember to call me with any questions."

I was grateful for all the support I'd received from my brother, Smitty, and Dr. Freilich, but the most important person to me was my wife. When I talked to Tina, I didn't let her see any of my anxiety because I didn't want to pass that on to her. Not only because I wanted to protect her, but I hid my concerns from my wife for myself as well. I knew if Tina saw how anxious I was, then I'd have to calm her down, too. At this moment I didn't have the capacity, I didn't have enough inside to tend to my wife's emotions while trying to deal with my own warring feelings. I knew Tina loved me and whatever I was feeling, she'd feel it, too. So I just gave Tina the facts straight, the way Dr. Chang had given them to me.

As I expected, everyone encouraged me, told me they would support whatever I decided, but no one gave me their opinion. They all said it had to be my decision, which I understood.

Over the next few days, while mulling over and measuring my options, I had to visit another doctor. While trying to determine if I was going to have this surgery, I had to visit Dr. Cykiert for a follow-up appointment from my cataract surgery that I'd had back in October 2015.

Dr. Cykiert was a cornea specialist I'd been seeing since I was a teen. He'd been referred to me by Dr. Topilow because I'd decided back then to wear contact lenses to help improve my sight and appearance. My first experience with Dr. Cykiert wasn't the best—the contact lenses he gave me didn't fit correctly; they were too tight, which caused my eye to redden.

From that point forward, I never really had a comfortable relationship with Dr. Cykiert but I stayed with him. I stayed with him because of Dr. Topilow.

Still, when I visited Dr. Cykiert for my six-month checkup, and he asked what was going on with me, I wanted to tell him so I could hear another doctor's opinion regarding Dr. Chang.

I filled Dr. Cykiert in on what had been happening with my vision, how I'd found out Dr. Topilow had passed away, and how I was now looking for my medical records because I'd found someone to perform the surgery.

"I was referred to one of the best doctors in the world to perform this surgery, Dr. Chang. Do you know him?"

One thing about Dr. Cykiert was that he always wore a stone face, never showing any emotions. His expression was blank when he said, "Yes, he's one of the top doctors, but," he paused and then hit me with a bombshell, "he's seventy!"

Now I was the one who had to pause for a moment. With the decision I had to make, this was what he was hitting me with now? My thoughts were spinning and just that quickly, I began doubting what everyone else had told me about Dr. Chang. Just like that, Dr. Cykiert had planted more than doubt. He filled me with confusion.

However, I didn't express any of that to him. All I said was, "You know what? That's a good point."

"I didn't even know that Dr. Chang was still practicing," he said, his voice filled with surprise.

"He is. And he seems to have a good reputation."

"He does." With a nod, Dr. Cykiert agreed. "His reputation is impeccable, but he's seventy," he repeated, just to make sure I hadn't missed it the first time he said it.

I sat there shocked by his response. Everyone else I'd spoken to only had one thing to say about Dr. Chang. That he was the best…period! Now here was Dr. Cykiert, the only one who had something negative to say.

I tried to shake off Dr. Cykiert's words. Of course, I was going with the advice of the doctors who talked about Dr. Chang's stellar reputation.

Then, I began wondering…maybe Dr. Cykiert knew something everyone else didn't know. It was true, Chang was older—could he perform this operation at seventy?

"Listen," Dr. Cykiert interrupted my thoughts, "I know someone who does this surgery; I want you to see my guy, Dr. Wald, and just get his opinion. He's got a lot of experience with your type of condition and second opinions are always good."

Dr. Cykiert finished his examination and sent me out of the office with a clean bill of health, at least as far as my cataract surgery was concerned. But if I thought I'd walked out of Dr. Chang's office anxious, I left Dr. Cykiert in a total state of confusion.

"But he's seventy!"

Dr. Cykiert's words played over and over in my mind. I really didn't know what to do now. The good thing was that I didn't have to make a decision—at least not until I saw Dr. Wald.

CHAPTER 6

Time was moving by and I didn't want too much to pass. So just four days after seeing Dr. Cykiert, I was in Dr. Wald's office. Like Dr. Cykiert had told me, Dr. Wald was much younger than Dr. Chang. That was my first thought when he walked into the room after the technician had done the preliminary tests. I guessed he was somewhere in his mid-forties. My next impression—Dr. Wald seemed like a young golden boy. It was everything about the doctor: his age, his aura, his looks. He could have been a star quarterback in his college days.

However, while he was younger and very professional, I quickly wondered if he was the right fit for me. His countenance seemed just a little off. Whenever I told a doctor about my history, every reaction was the same: You've had eight retinal detachments, four in each eye, ten surgeries altogether, and your right eye is a prosthetic?

There was always shock and awe from the other doctors, but not from Dr. Wald. He just smiled. The entire time I shared my medical bio with him—he smiled. When I told him what the other doctors said—he smiled. He smiled the whole time, as if I was telling a story he'd heard before. Nothing I said seemed to surprise him or impress him. He was weirdly jovial the entire time.

When I finished, Dr. Wald said, "Well, I can do the surgery." Then, just as Dr. Chang had done a week ago, Dr. Wald gave me the pros and cons of having this surgery. "It's likely to be successful, but there are no guarantees. And the biggest thing is that at the end of the surgery, your healing will be up to you."

He told me how I'd have to keep my head in a face-down position and, once again, I felt the pressure of my healing being on my shoulders…literally.

"Keeping your head down is critical to the healing process," he said, repeating Dr. Chang's exact words. Then, he put even more pressure on me when he told me what I'd already been feeling. "It's all on you because if you don't do this effectively, then the surgery will not be a success."

The doctor continued to talk about how the gas bubble worked and told me about another alternative—using silicone oil, where I wouldn't have to keep my head down as much.

"But that would require a second surgery," he explained. "A surgery to take out the oil."

As he kept on explaining the complications, I thought how Dr. Chess had said my eye was a land mine. From everything Dr. Wald was saying, Dr. Chess had been correct. If that was true—if my eye was a land mine—then maybe Dr. Cykiert was correct. Dr. Wald wasn't seventy, and that fact alone might make him the better choice for such a risky surgery.

Dr. Wald broke through the debate going on in my head. "There is one thing, though. I can do the surgery, but I'm not even sure we have the instruments to perform this on your eye."

"What do you mean?"

He gave me a little lesson on eyeballs. The average eye is round and somewhere between twenty-three to twenty-six millimeters. Dr. Wald explained that my eye's shape was more oblong; it was elongated and about thirty-seven millimeters. That was what caused my high myopia, and that was what made my retina more susceptible to the rips and tears I'd suffered over the years.

"But I'd love to do this surgery. So let's do it," Dr. Wald said.

After asking him a few more questions, mostly about keeping my head down, I left his office without committing, but with having a new piece of information—they might not have the instruments to perform the surgery on me. This situation just kept getting more complicated as now, I had another decision to make.

Was I going to do this with seventy-year-old Dr. Chang, one of the best in the world, or was I going to go with the younger golden boy, Dr. Wald?

As I thought about it, I had a third choice, too. With the success of the surgery firmly on my shoulders, I could have decided not to do anything. I could have decided not to take the chance, hoping this didn't get any worse.

I sighed as I rolled over all three options in my mind. At that moment, I truly didn't know what I was going to do. This was going to take a lot more prayer.

CHAPTER 7

Dr. Wald telling me about the instruments really hit home just how serious this was going to be. "I'm not even sure we have the instruments to perform this surgery on your eye."

That was hard to believe and now, I wondered what would happen if I did the surgery and then they couldn't find the instruments? What would happen to me if I couldn't have the operation because I was the only guy in the world with a problem like this?

After leaving Dr. Wald, I went home and talked to Tina. Like always, I told her everything: how Dr. Wald had gone into a lot more detail about keeping my head down for ten days; how he'd given me more information about the gas bubble, which was the key to the surgery being successful; and what he'd said about the instruments.

"So what happens if keeping your head down doesn't work?" Tina asked.

"That's what I asked Dr. Wald. Because I'm really worried about being able to do that properly. So I asked him what were the risks, and he explained that if the gas bubble didn't work, they would put silicon oil in. But if they use silicon oil, they'll have to do another surgery to take the silicon oil out, whereas, with the gas bubble, it just dissolves."

"So with the silicon oil, you wouldn't have to hold your head down?"

"Not as strictly as with the gas bubble."

I could see Tina thinking about that. "So, why wouldn't they just go ahead and use the silicone oil?"

"They'd rather not because it would require a second surgery. And since surgeries are always risky, they don't want to do a second one if they don't have to."

She nodded, exactly the way I'd done when Dr. Wald told me that. The less they had to cut into my eye, the better off I'd be. His words had made sense to me then, and now I could tell it made sense to Tina, too.

I could tell, though, that she had just as many questions as I had, but she didn't have the answers. This decision would be totally on me. The only thing my wife wanted to give me was support. She would be by my side no matter which way I went.

I knew this was not a decision I could make alone. I was a spiritual person, especially once I entered the 12-step program many years before. My journey in the program helped me to fill the void that had first caused me to use drugs. The step work done in the program was based on spiritual principles and designed to help stop self-destructive attitudes and behaviors.

Once I understood the spiritual principles, I stopped relying on my will and started relying on God's will. Since that time, I'd been staying close to God and now, there was no better time for me to, once again, take my concerns to Him.

At that point, this became a very spiritual process for me. So, I connected again with Dr. Freilich because I felt he could help. I had no point of reference between Dr. Chang and Dr. Wald, but Dr. Freilich knew them both. Of all the doctors I'd seen during this process, I trusted Dr. Freilich the most. After what he'd done to connect me to Dr. Chang, I knew he wanted the best care for me. That was his bottom line.

I called Dr. Freilich and while he wasn't available then, he got right back to me. I told him about my visit to Dr. Wald, how I felt about him, what he'd said about the instruments, and the information about the silicon oil and the second surgery. Then I repeated what Dr. Cykiert had said about Dr. Chang's age.

"So with all of that, Dr. Freilich, what do you think I should do?"

Even before I finished asking, I knew Dr. Freilich wasn't going to answer that question directly. Not only would he never criticize one doctor over another, but he also would never tell me what to do.

"I get it. This is a tough decision. Yes, Chang is seventy. And is Dr. Wald good? Yes to that, too. But while I can't tell you what to do, I can tell you that if it were me, I would go with the best guy in the world."

It was that simple. Dr. Freilich was right. It was time to end the emotional stress of going back and forth. I decided to move forward with the best guy in the world.

The next day I called Dr. Chang's office, and the receptionist told me Dr. Chang was in surgery. I knew that;

Dr. Chang did all of his surgeries on Tuesdays. However, he called me right back between operations and set me up with his surgical coordinator.

Once I pulled that trigger and told Dr. Chang I was ready to go, I was under the gun because we were working on Dr. Chang's tight timetable. The surgical coordinator scheduled me for the following Tuesday, just a week away, because Dr. Chang was leaving the country and he wanted to have enough time after the surgery to be there for the majority of my healing process.

There was so much I had to do in just a week. First up, I had to get medical clearance from my primary care doctor, making sure my heart was healthy and I was good for surgery. That wasn't an easy feat; I had to get squeezed in for that appointment.

Then, there was ordering all the contraptions that were necessary for my recovery: the chair, the pillows, everything I'd needed to support my two weeks of walking around with my head down.

I felt like it was all moving so fast. However, even though I was scrambling, I felt a certain peace…if that was the word. It was hard to describe exactly what I was feeling, but it reminded me of my mindset when my mom passed away. When it first happened, of course, I was filled with grief. But I didn't panic, I didn't break down. I was the youngest of her three children, but I was the one who took care of it all. My heart was heavy, but I had a kind of serene strength that allowed me to push forward and get everything done.

This felt exactly the same way. I had that kind of peace; I had that kind of strength. Yes, I still had uncertainty about the surgery and its outcome, but I had enough peace to handle the business. So, along with Tina, who was a big part of this because she helped me get everything in order, we teamed up and got it done. She went to work, setting up my doctor's appointment, and I made the calls to order the equipment.

Once I had that done, I had to handle my business at my office. As the Vice President in charge of the Canadian division at a major credit card processing company, my absence was going to be noticeable. Speaking with Alex, a partner of the firm, was easy enough. I'd already told him I needed this surgery.

"I'll probably be out for a month. But after the first week, I should be able to work from home."

Being able to get back to work as soon as possible was really important to me. After the surgery, work would connect me to some sense of normalcy. There was no way I'd be able to sit home with my head down, doing nothing. I'd go stir crazy.

So at home, with my mobile phone and ear buds, I would certainly be able to talk. My support staff at the office could communicate with me, and I'd get all the information I needed to get the work done. Plus, I'd been doing it for so long—I could do it with my eyes closed.

Alex was totally fine with my having to take some time off. He repeated what he'd told me before. "Look, Steve, it is what it is."

That was his way of showing support and, once again, I reassured him I didn't plan for my department to miss a beat.

Once that was settled with Alex, I met with my staff. I wasn't going to share the depth of what I was going through—

and that was on purpose. I didn't want anyone to panic or worry about me. I didn't want any kind of sympathy.

"I have to have eye surgery and I'll be out for several weeks. But I'll be working from home, so with your support, it will all go well."

That was the pep talk I gave them, but the prospect of my being gone for so long was a lot for everyone to process. I knew there were people in the company who expected my staff to slack off in my absence, but I didn't. I knew they would do well, and I told them I believed in every one of them. (By the way, we did well. Production actually increased slightly.)

Once I had all of that covered, it was time for me to get focused on myself, my mind, and the surgery. It was time for my weekend of prayer, meditation, and affirmations to begin.

CHAPTER 8

I had given myself a three-day weekend because I wanted Saturday, Sunday, and Monday to be a time of mental and spiritual peace before I went into what would be the most important surgery of my life.

When the weekend came, that was what I felt—a sense of peace. Of course, there was a little bit of fear inside of me. That was residual emotions left over from all the surgeries I'd had up to this point and knowing any kind of surgery was risky.

But I once heard a wonderful saying: Courage is not the absence of fear—courage is pressing forward in the midst of fear.

That was the truth.

I was pressing forward through all of my fears because the alternative wasn't acceptable. What was I going to do? Crawl into a corner? Just cower and let this beat me?

No! I was going to fight, and I was going to fight with my faith. We say God is good all the time, but do we really mean that? Or do we mean God is only good when things are good? Which one is it?

My answer: God is good all the time and even when things don't look peachy, He is still good. Even when you're up against the wall, He is still good. That was what I was going to remember.

Even though this was what I knew in my heart, other thoughts seeped into my mind that made the weekend a little bit tough. I needed to fill my head with hope; I needed my faith strengthened. I was looking for all the unseen elements that one needs to go through to get through. I needed God's comforting presence to be upon me, and He sent the people to give me that. It came to me through whispers from the ones I reached out to.

I started with my brother and Smitty like I always did. Next, I reached out to Fernando and Orlando, other men in my life with a strong spiritual foundation and filled with wisdom. Each of the men delivered their message to me in a different way, but the message was consistent and clear— God's got you, God's got this. I hung up from all of them, feeling wrapped in a blanket of peace.

The best part of the weekend, though, was having Tina there with me. This was a big deal for me, so that meant it was a big deal for her. I was grateful my wife had a support system of her own. We had a lot of friends through a couples' group Tina and I started—Complete Chocolate Couples. It was a Meetup group dedicated to celebrating and empowering healthy and positive relationships in our communities. There were four hundred couples in the group and often we would do things together: go out to dinner, attend sporting events, hang out and participate in recreational activities, or any activity that couples would do alone, we did as a group.

Within that group, we'd developed some strong friendships and stayed in touch beyond just the couples' meetings. We texted and spoke to each other in-between our get-togethers, so some couples were very aware of my upcoming surgery.

Over the weekend, my wife's phone constantly rang with calls and texts from the women and their husbands who sent their prayers and love to both of us.

That was what the weekend was about—days filled with lots of love and hope and the reminder that God was still and would always be in control. There was a positive affirmation I said every morning—God, thank you for Your comforting presence upon me—and He delivered His comforting presence to me and my wife through the people in our lives.

The day before my surgery, that Monday was even quieter than the weekend. I spent a lot of time alone, just being quiet, being still, and speaking to God.

I also took the time to reach out to other people. Though consumed with thoughts and feelings about my surgery the next day, some of our friends were going through challenges of their own. One couple was trying to have a baby, and they were having complications—so Tina and I prayed with them. Then, another friend had just lost his son. Tina and I called and prayed with him and his wife. Another good friend of ours had just gone through a miscarriage, so Tina and I called and prayed with her.

All of our friends were taken aback that the day before my surgery I would reach out to them. Of course, I would. I cared about each of them and wanted to give my support. But also, in my own way, I was sending out positive energy and trusting that it would come back to me. Praying with others reinforced my faith, and these were friends who needed Tina and me in this capacity.

I was trying not to be so caught up in my own situation. They were all so appreciative of us reaching out. That pleased me, and I was sure it pleased God, too.

On Monday evening, there was nothing left to do except settle into the peace that God had given to me through my friends. But He was not finished with me yet.

In the middle of the calm that I was feeling, my wife said to me, "You know Cousin Stephanie wants to pray with you. It's getting late, so we need to call her."

My wife's cousin, Stephanie, was always a bright light in our lives. It was more than just her outgoing personality, it was also her faith. She was a woman who devoutly believed in God and the power of prayer. Being around her, you could feel her love for God.

Stephanie had told my wife that she and her Sister in Christ, Evangelist Jessup, wanted to pray with me, and Evangelist Jessup was a prayer warrior for sure. I was grateful that both women wanted to pray for and share this time with me.

Since it was getting late, I told my wife, "Let's do it."

We got the two ladies on the phone and from the moment we heard their voices, I smiled. They got right to the business at hand; the two of them prayed for me in earnest, asking God to bless me, to bless the doctors, to bless everything. They filled me with even more peace...if that was possible.

When we hung up that phone, I was definitely prayed up and ready for tomorrow.

CHAPTER 9

From the moment I found out I had to have this surgery, I'd developed a ritual where every night I'd go into the living room, turn off the lights, and then, after quieting my mind from all the noise of the day and the noise of my thoughts, I would commune with God. I spent that time in concentrated prayer, meditation, and affirmation.

I would repeat the same words, "Thank you, God, for a successful surgery. Thank you, that my eye is healed. Thank you, that my vision is 20/20."

I was speaking into existence what I couldn't see. I believed my affirmations had already worked; I was sure this was the reason I was connected to Dr. Chang. What were my chances of getting one of the best doctors in the world? The chances of that happening were slim, so I knew it was my faith, my trust, and my actions that drew Dr. Chang to me. I had no doubt about this.

The next morning when Tina and I left for Columbia Presbyterian Hospital, I was prayed up and ready. I had no second thoughts. I just wanted to get it done.

As Tina drove to the hospital, I put in my earbuds and listened to meditation music I'd downloaded. In my mind, I chanted my affirmations. I chanted victory over the surgery.

The routine, once we arrived at the hospital, was so familiar to me. Memories of past surgeries raced through my mind as we checked in at the front and told the attendants at the Information Desk that we were going to the 7th floor for my surgery that morning.

When the elevator doors opened, a West Indian woman met us and took us into her small office, and logged us into the system.

"You haven't had anything to eat or drink in the last twelve hours, have you?"

"No." I had followed the instructions given to me by the surgical coordinator.

She secured the band with my name and other information onto my wrist, and then Tina and I were taken into a private room where I was prepped for surgery.

The nurses who came in and out of the room seemed focused on making me feel comfortable and calm—and it worked. They all spoke to me with a lilt in their voices and melody in their tones. They definitely lightened the mood.

I changed into the surgical gown, then washed my face with the cloth and soap given to me. I was used to that—there couldn't be any kind of lotion or oil on my face.

When the nurses left us alone, Tina and I waited in silence. My wife was on her phone, texting back all the people who were still checking in with her. I could tell she was trying to control her own emotions, just as I was trying to do the same with mine. That was how we supported each other.

While Tina was on her phone, I received a couple of calls myself. My daughters and son called, wishing me good luck. Hearing their voices was soothing as I waited.

Then, "Hello, Mr. King."

I glanced up. This was the first time a male nurse had come to assist me.

"I'm going to just take your vitals, but before I do that, what's your name and date of birth?"

Even though he'd just called me Mr. King, I answered, and I guessed my answers were correct because he proceeded to take my vitals, then began filling my eyes with a barrage of eye drops. This was something else I was used to—the eye drops came in four sets…they'd give me drops, wait ten minutes, then give me a new set. The drops were for a couple of things: antibiotics to make sure I didn't get an infection, another drop was to dilate my eye, and a few drops were nerve-blockers, like local anesthetics because I would be awake during the entire surgery.

In about an hour or so, another nurse finally entered with a wheelchair. In the past, I'd been taken to the operating room on a gurney, but so many things had changed over the decades.

After she asked my name and date of birth, I settled into the wheelchair. Then I asked Tina, "Do you have my phone?"

She nodded.

"Do you have my wallet?"

She nodded again. "I have everything," she said, her way of telling me to shut down the questioning. She had it all.

Of course, my wife had everything under control. But I'm from Harlem, so I always had my eye on everything—even when that eye was about to be operated on.

I kissed Tina before I took that familiar roll down the hospital's halls. At the elevator, I took a deep breath—it was showtime.

Inside the operating room, I was met with more that was familiar—the sight of the medical team, all in surgical gear. The sounds of the machines, some beeping, some whirring, and then that antiseptic smell.

Before I scooted onto the table, a nurse had given me a pair of black compression socks to reduce any circulation issues in my legs during the surgery. This reminded me of how the surgery would affect my entire body. Then, they attached the monitors to me before wrapping me in a warm blanket and covering my head with the shower-type cap.

"What's your name and date of birth?"

It was almost comical the way everyone asked me that, though it was for a very serious, and very good, reason. So many people, so many surgeries—at every point they had to make sure they had the right one.

"Do you want another blanket?" one nurse asked.

"No, I'm good." I took another calming breath.

Next, it was the anesthesiologist who asked me to identify myself before he went through the protocol with me.

"You won't be asleep," the doctor told me. "You'll be given sedatives, but you will be awake. You'll be somewhat aware, but this is just to relax you."

This was where this surgery was going to differ from the others. In the past, I'd always been asleep, under general anesthesia, except for the cataract surgery I'd had in October 2015. I had to admit, the thought of being awake made me a bit anxious. It was hard to fathom being conscious while Dr. Chang was operating on my eye.

58

"Hello, Steve." I recognized his voice before I even saw Dr. Chang. "We'll be starting in a few minutes."

Dr. Chang didn't ask my name and birthdate, but he did take out a pen and made a mark on my forehead above my left eye. I wondered if he had drawn an arrow, a sign to himself. That was funny, especially since I thought it was so elemental—just a pen, just a mark, on my forehead.

"This should take about an hour, okay?" Dr. Chang said, though I was sure he wasn't asking my permission.

With the oxygen mask covering my face, I knew it was time. I felt like I was in a movie where the patient was on the operating table and all the moviegoers saw were the faces of the medical team looking down at the patient. That's how it was for me—only in slow motion.

It must have been the sedatives they had given me. I was way more than just relaxed, but definitely aware. I knew what was going on; I could hear, but with my senses dulled, I couldn't react.

There was a bright light above me and, for a moment, it took me back to those first examinations when the light blinded me completely. The light from the bulb above was bright like that, but it wasn't blinding this time.

"How are you doing, Steve?" Dr. Chang asked.

"I'm fine."

I was telling the truth; I was fine, though I felt weird. I could see the shadow of Dr. Chang's instruments inside my eye as he worked. I couldn't feel anything, though, so I didn't panic. Still, it was a strange sensation.

I don't know how much more time passed before Dr. Chang asked again, "How are you doing, Steve?"

59

Again, I told him I was fine, but then, right after that, Dr. Chang said to his assistant, "We have to try this once again."

I wondered what that meant. Was there something wrong? I didn't have any concept of time, but it felt like more than an hour had passed. That had to mean that something was wrong.

I didn't react, though. I didn't panic; I guessed it was the drugs. I began to feel a bit of pressure in my eye. It wasn't painful, but it felt as if Dr. Chang was digging, trying to reach something.

Dr. Wald's words came back to me: "I'm not even sure we have the instruments to perform this surgery on your eye."

Finally, Dr. Chang said, "Okay, Steve, we're getting ready to put the gas bubble in."

I exhaled a sigh of relief; this meant he was close to the end. Dr. Chang instructed his resident as he performed this part of the operation.

Then finally, "Steve, we're done," Dr. Chang said. After a pause, he added, "This was a tough one, but we got it done."

One of the most successful doctors in the world had just said that about my operation.

A nurse wrapped my eye in gauze and another detached me from all the monitors. With assistance, I was back in the wheelchair and rolled through the hall and into the elevator, during which time I reflected on the fact that after all these weeks of angst, my surgery was over.

Once I was inside the room, I couldn't see, but I knew Tina was right there. I could feel her before she even spoke.

As the nurse helped me into bed, Tina asked, "How are you feeling?"

"I feel good."

The nurse said, "Well, you have Dr. Chang, and he's the best doctor in the world. He's amazing."

I wondered how many times I'd heard that already. Still, every time I heard it, I felt just as grateful as the first time.

The nurse left us alone, and I felt Tina hovering near. When she took my hand, I felt comforted.

Moments later, the nurse returned to the room. "Okay, I have this for you. Juice and crackers. Drink this, eat those and then relax until you're ready."

That juice and those crackers helped, and it wasn't long before I felt fully conscious and ready to get dressed. But I couldn't see anything, and I had to keep my head down. This was the part that was going to be so awkward, so different, but this was the part that would determine the success of the surgery. So Tina had to help me do everything.

The nurse returned to the room with a set of eye drops and the instructions on how to take them—how many drops and how often. Just as she finished, Dr. Chang came in.

After greeting Tina and me and then asking how I felt, Dr. Chang repeated what he'd said in the operating room. "This was a tough one, but we got it done."

"How long did it take?"

"It took a little bit longer—about an hour and a half," he said, sounding as straightforward as he did when he was in his office. He was never as warm as the other staff members, but that had nothing to do with me; that was just his way. He really cared and that was apparent in not only the way he'd scheduled me in so I could get his maximum care, but in the way he asked how I was doing.

Dr. Chang reiterated all the instructions about keeping my head down, sleeping only on one side, keeping my eye covered for the night, no showering yet, and just practicing extreme caution.

Dr. Chang then said, "Just relax and come and see me tomorrow morning and I'll let you know all the other things that you have to do."

All the other things? I felt like I'd received so many instructions already, but whatever he wanted to add, I was definitely ready.

Except, I found out that I was not ready at all. Since my first meeting with Dr. Chang, I knew I'd have to keep my head down and I'd imagined how difficult that would be. What I didn't expect was the strain it would place on my neck.

I felt it on the ride home, starting as a little constant ache. It progressed and hurt so much that I couldn't wait to lay down.

When we got home, I felt so much relief that the ride was over. It was still fairly early in the day; a bit after noon. All I wanted to do, though, was lay down. I wanted to relieve the ache in my neck, but not only that, I was more mentally exhausted than I'd expected.

As I lay down, I had two thoughts: I was really tired, and I was so grateful for Tina.

My wife was so caring, so cautious and because I couldn't see anything, I was so appreciative she was there not only with me, but also there for me.

As much as I tried, nothing could have prepared me. I never imagined how really difficult the next two weeks would be.

CHAPTER 10

I wasn't sure how long I'd slept. Without sight, it was hard to have a sense of time because I couldn't judge by the daylight. I didn't think it had been too long. It had been difficult to get comfortable since so many questions occupied my head. First, I wondered if I was laying down on the right side, with my head in the right position. I didn't know why it confused me, but it was like suddenly I couldn't remember exactly what I was to do. Then, my mind became filled with thoughts and questions about whether the surgery had gone well. Was this going to be all right?

I tried to stay in bed and just listen to the sounds of my life. From the living room, I heard Tina's cell phone ringing. It didn't seem to stop, so I knew folks were calling to check on me. Even though she kept her voice low, not wanting to disturb me, I still heard many of her words. It was as if not having sight heightened my sense of hearing.

Beyond Tina's conversations, though, my focus was mostly on the darkness and it was frightening. After a couple of hours, I couldn't stay in bed anymore. The sedative from the surgery had pretty much worn off and, although I was still mentally exhausted, I didn't physically feel as tired as when I'd come home. It didn't make much sense for me to continue laying down, anyway. Laying in the dark this way was going to drive me crazy.

When I rolled myself up and sat on the bed, I realized something…I was going to have to learn how to do everything with my head down. Of course, I knew this all along, but now, reality had just hit me. The good thing was, I wasn't in any pain. All I could say was that it felt weird—not being able to see and having to hold my head down, but this was the beginning of a strange new process.

Now that I was up, I called out to Tina and as she rushed to me, I once again thanked God for her. This was going to take some getting used to—me completely relying on my wife. But while that was scary, Tina made me feel safe. She made me feel protected, nurtured…just completely secure in her care.

Still, it was unnerving; this went against my being the protector and the provider. The fear stayed in the back of my mind—was this the way it was going to be?

When Tina came into the bedroom, she was extra cautious, gripping my arm, posturing herself so she could catch me if I fell. She led me to the bathroom first, positioning me in front of the toilet. When I finished, she guided me to the sink to wash my hands where the eucalyptus fragrance from the soap filled the bathroom.

It felt like a journey from the bathroom to the living room sofa, and once I sat down, I realized how much I'd taken for granted. I'd never thought going to the bathroom would be a challenge to navigate, and now, I had to figure out how I was going to master the art of eating without being able to see.

Tina placed the plate in front of me, then put the food on my fork before she handed the fork to me. At least I could feed myself.

Even though I knew I would need help, this was unbelievable.

"How are you doing?" Tina asked in the middle of my meal. I told her I was fine and then…that was it. She didn't say another word.

Her silence made me wonder what was going on with my wife. Tina being quiet was completely opposite her normal personality. I always teased her about how she chattered about everything—one of the things that I love about her.

However, there was no chatter now. She was quiet, as if she didn't want to disturb me, not even with her words. Yet, she was right there, at my beck and call, for anything I wanted. Even in her silence, though, I felt her concern. I knew she was worried about me.

After dinner, I wanted to sit in the chair for a while. I hadn't tried that yet, and since we had set the chair up in the living room, I wouldn't have to go far. The chair was unusual, almost like a massage chair with a pillow where I rested my head, face down.

We'd set it up so I could watch, or rather listen, to the TV. I positioned myself in the chair and sitting that way felt good for a while. It relieved the pressure in my neck, but except for that, the chair wasn't all that comfortable.

It didn't take long before all I wanted to do was go back to bed. I called out to Tina, and she helped me get up, then we maneuvered our way from the living room, through the hallway, to the bedroom, and finally into bed. This time, though, I was so tired that finally, I slept.

When I opened my eyes, I figured it was morning. Without light, without being able to see a clock, I couldn't tell for sure. Whatever the time, it was early because Tina was still asleep.

I'd been in and out of consciousness all night; mostly concerned about whether I was sleeping correctly. I'd made it through this surgery, I certainly didn't want to mess it up by sleeping the wrong way.

Taking a deep breath, I tried to calm my thoughts and settle down so I could pray. I wanted to stay in that space of gratefulness because there was so much for me to be thankful for. After almost twenty-four hours, I was on the other side of surgery.

I lay there in the darkness, thinking, reflecting, and wanting to counteract any negativity that tried to seep into my mind. It was hard to keep the negativity away, but I refused to beat myself up. I was human and walking in unchartered and very scary territory.

When the alarm finally rang, I felt more than relief. Now, I felt a bit eager to get up and get out so we could get to Dr. Chang's office. I was eager to hear that everything had gone fine with my surgery.

Just like the day before, I had to rely on Tina for everything, including getting dressed. But this was one place where I had things a bit under control. When it came to my clothes, I was meticulous, almost to the level of OCD. My closet and my drawers were so organized; I'd lined up everything in order by color and by clothes items. In the past, I'd teased Tina about her having spousal hate when it came to my closet, but right now, we were both grateful for my organizational skills. I could direct Tina to everything I wanted to wear for the beautiful May day. I gave her instructions, even down to my belt.

It was so early, we left without eating. That was fine with me because I wanted to get to Dr. Chang's office. However, the moment Tina opened the front door of our apartment, anxiety rushed over me. My wife held onto me with a tight grip, as if she never planned to let me go, guiding me, helping me—and, once again, there was so much comfort in that, even as it felt scary to be walking completely without sight. As we moved down the hallway, I challenged myself, counting the steps that I'd taken thousands of times.

"How are you doing?" Tina asked as we took slow, tentative steps.

"I'm fine." I held onto her, trying to feel my way at the same time.

After that, we didn't exchange too many more words. Tina just wanted to make sure I was okay, and I wanted to assure her I was. However, when we finally got settled into the car, I felt nothing close to okay. I felt frustrated and frightened, not at all like myself.

Before Tina started the car, she asked, "Are you okay?" and just like that, the sound of her voice calmed me again.

On the ride to the doctor's office, the silence between us continued. I felt like Tina was on guard, walking on eggshells.

She would only talk after I spoke. I had little to say because just a few minutes into the drive to Dr. Chang's office on 53rd Street, I began to feel the strain in my neck. It had just been twenty-four hours and already this was getting to me. It wasn't painful, but I felt extreme discomfort, a discomfort that, with everything inside of me, I wanted to raise my head and ease.

The questions that rolled through my mind didn't help either: Was I holding my head right? Was my head tilted down far enough?

I had no barometer of what was right and what was wrong. All I had were questions that were creating anxiety on top of all the anxiety I already had.

The ride to Dr. Chang's office took about an hour and I was glad when we arrived, just to walk a bit and relieve the pressure on my neck. However, once I slid out of the car, I quickly realized there would be no relief from the pressure. I was also blanketed with a heavy feeling of self-consciousness.

This was the first time I'd have to maneuver outside. That made me feel vulnerable, especially with the way Tina had to hold me and with the patch that covered my eye. It was clear to anyone who looked at us that I was dependent on my wife.

As we moved through the parking garage toward the exit, I wondered what the parking attendant thought as we walked away. I wondered about the other people in the garage—what did they see when they looked at me and Tina?

Then suddenly, I felt a shift in the atmosphere. The sounds of the city were louder. I could feel the presence of more people. We had stepped out of the garage and onto the street. If I hadn't noticed all of that, I would have certainly noticed the way Tina held me, now a little tighter, and her directions were more frequent.

"Step down here."

"Step up there."

"We're at a light, we're going to wait."

She was like a lioness; I felt her protection. She was cautious but thorough. My wife had me; I was in good hands.

"Okay, we're getting ready to walk into the building," Tina said.

I remembered the lobby, and I tried to imagine everyone I'd seen before—from the security guard to the women at the information desk. I heard the security guard greet us, and I wondered what he thought. When we stepped into the elevator, I wondered what the people who were in there with us were thinking.

When the elevator doors opened and we stepped out, I took a deep breath, trying to shift my thoughts. But it didn't work. As Tina led me to Dr. Chang's office, all I could think was, I'm blind. I really can't see anything.

That thought had been looming in the back of my mind, but now that I was about to see Dr. Chang, being blind was all I could think about. What if I found out that the operation didn't work? If it hadn't, this was going to be my life.

With another deep breath, I shook those thoughts away. There was no reason for me to imagine these worst-case scenarios. In a few minutes, we'd see Dr. Chang, and then I'd have some answers.

CHAPTER 11

Inside Dr. Chang's office, Tina spoke to the receptionist, and though I couldn't see her, I heard the sympathy in the softness of her voice as she said, "Okay, Dr. Chang will be right with you."

Just like the security guard and the people in the lobby, I knew the receptionist had seen thousands of patients like me. But at this moment, what was going on with me and her reaction was my only focus.

As I sat, Tina had to sign some papers, and once again, my neck was aching. If I was going through this after just one day, I couldn't imagine what the next two weeks would be like.

Dr. Chang didn't have us waiting for very long. One of Dr. Chang's nurses called us in and I released a sigh of relief when I sat in the examination chair.

"How did you do through the night?" the nurse asked me. "Any pain in the eye?"

"No, I've been good," I said, thinking I'd save my major questions for the doctor.

"Dr. Chang will be in with you in a minute."

The moment we were alone, Tina asked, "Are you okay?"

"Yeah, I'm good."

Then that was it. Tina went back to her unusual silence. It didn't last long because, within minutes, Dr. Chang came into the room.

"Hello, Steve. Hello, Tina." It seemed like he was more chipper, more upbeat this morning...his lighter mood was encouraging.

As he removed the gauze from my eye, he asked me a bunch of questions.

"So, how do you feel, Steve?"

"Do you have any pain?"

"How did you sleep?"

With the gauze removed, I still couldn't see anything because of the gas bubble. The bubble, with its purplish tint, felt like looking through a glass of grape Kool-Aid. Even though it was liquid, I couldn't see through it; although the bubble did move, giving me the feeling of having waves in my eye.

Dr. Chang shone the coal miner's light in my eye and I felt the heat of it, but I couldn't see the light. Then, he gently cleaned my eye with a gauze pad that was soaked in a sterile solution.

"The surgery went well," Dr. Chang repeated what he'd told me the day before. "It took a little longer, but, it went well." After another moment, he clicked off the light. "Everything looks good."

I exhaled as Dr. Chang wrapped my eye with fresh gauze and a protective shell, and once again, he reviewed the regiment of the drops I had to take. Four drops: a steroid for inflammation, an antibiotic, and drops for pressure. They all had distinctive colors on the caps, so it would be easy for Tina to identify which one was for what.

"You'll have to take each four times a day," he instructed again. "Once you get home, you can take the gauze off. You won't need it anymore."

That wasn't a big deal to me. Even with removing the gauze, I still wouldn't be able to see. Dr. Chang also told me I'd have to wear the plastic shell at all times, even when I was asleep. That was for protection against objects hitting my eye so nothing would happen in the middle of the night, like Tina rolling over and bumping me.

When Dr. Chang was finished with his questions and instructions, I had a list of things I wanted to know: How exactly should I lay in bed? How should I bathe? What else did I need to know to protect my eye?

With the patience he always had, Dr. Chang answered all of my questions. Finally, he said, "All right, Steve. At this point, I'm pleased. Everything looks good. There's no hemorrhaging, and that's a great sign. Just remember to keep your head down and I'll see you next Monday."

His words were comforting; it was going well.

The entire visit was about a half-hour, with about ten minutes with Dr. Chang. That's how he was—in and out.

We scheduled the next appointment with the receptionist and I was glad I was coming back so soon. It seemed Dr. Chang was keeping me on a short leash, which I appreciated. He was going to be with me every step of the way.

That ended the first post-op visit. Now I could officially begin the second part of the journey.

CHAPTER 12

It had just been a visit to the doctor's office, but being out and about was taxing. Yesterday when I traveled home right after the surgery, I had the benefit of the sedative. Today, there was nothing to ease the discomfort in my neck during this ride in the car, and all I wanted to do was get home quickly.

Even though I was agitated, I didn't want to show my emotions or any feelings to Tina. So instead of thinking about my discomfort, I tried to focus on all that was going on around me. I used my other senses to figure out where we were just by the turns we were making and the sounds that I heard. I noticed when we were in traffic, then the change of the sounds as we entered the Lincoln Tunnel. I could tell when we made it to the other side and were in New Jersey.

When we made it home and were in the garage, Tina was, once again, my loving, caring, cautious wife. Every time I heard her voice or felt her arm interlocked in mine, it comforted me in the middle of my frustration or agitation.

We took the same slow steps down the long hallway toward our apartment, and I counted my steps as I felt my way using the wall. I wanted to master my surroundings. Not that I would walk down this hall alone in the next two weeks, but feeling as if I could do it gave me a little sense of independence.

Stepping into our apartment, I breathed deeply, feeling as if I had achieved a victory. I'd made it.

"Are you hungry?" Tina asked. "Do you want something to eat?"

I was hungry, but I told Tina I wanted to lay down for a little while to take the pressure off of my neck. Inside the bedroom, she turned on the TV to a news station and I tried to rest as the political pundits chatted away about the new president's first days in office. My thoughts didn't stay on the new president, though. Instead, my mind drifted to what the next two weeks were going to be like. Would I be able to keep my head down all of that time, even with the pressure? Would I be able to handle that strain?

Finally, between the news and my thoughts, I dozed off. I wasn't sure how long I slept before the alarm on my phone woke me. At first, that was a little disorienting, until Tina came into the bedroom.

"It's time for your drops," she said as she helped me from the bed. "You can go back to sleep afterward, but you can't miss the drops."

We had decided before that the bathroom was the best place for Tina to put the drops into my eyes. The bathroom's light was bright, so that would make it easier for her, especially since I could use the commode as a seat and she could just stand above me.

I had thought this task would be easy enough. I'd had to use eye drops of some sort for so much of my life. It was just that I couldn't do it myself this time. However, it wasn't as easy for Tina. She had never done anything like this, and as I held my head back, I could tell how cautious she was trying to be.

She missed the mark a few times, and the drops ended up getting nowhere close to my eye and dripped down my cheek instead. After a few more tries, she got the hang of it.

Once done, Tina covered my eye with the plastic shell that was just a little thicker than a black eye patch, but much harder. She secured it over my eye with surgical tape before she led me back into the bedroom.

"Do you want to lay back down?" she asked.

Tired of laying down, it was time for me to figure out how I was going to make it over the next two weeks. I went into the living room and sat in the chair for a while. Like the day before, it took the pressure off my neck, but the chair felt uncomfortable. I think it was my height that made it so awkward. It didn't feel as if the chair was made for someone over six feet tall. Just a few minutes later, I moved to the sofa.

Tina had ordered a sandwich and fries for me from Good Eats, a place that would become our regular eatery. That was the highlight of the day so far, especially since, while eating, I could distinguish between the sandwich and the fries.

After I ate, I got into a little bit of a routine where I would lay on the sofa, then get up and sit in the chair. Between, Tina would put the drops in my eye. It didn't feel like I was doing much, but by the time I went to bed, I was ready for the day to be over. At least we'd made it through the first full day.

The good thing about the next day was that I was ready to begin living just a little more of my life and that would start with my job. Very quickly, I got set up—as I sat in the chair, I could use my phone. The Siri command on my phone became my best friend; I'd be able to make calls, check voicemails, send and listen to text messages—all without having to see.

The good thing about getting "back" to work was that it took my focus away from my situation. Now I could turn my paranoia to the job. It had only been four days, but I was afraid of business falling off without me. I wanted to check in with the office to find out what was going on and to see if I could be of any help and support them in any way.

The moment I heard Cora, my assistant and liaison to the outside reps, I knew if things weren't going okay, she wouldn't tell me. From the tone in her voice, I could tell she was far more concerned about me than anything going on in the office.

I tried to keep the attention on business, asking about the numbers, wanting to know if anyone had any issues and if any deals had come in during the four days I'd been away. It must have been the way I was speaking—I sounded fine to her, so finally, she gave me a full update and report.

After I checked in with my assistant, I took a few calls from the reps in the field. That was all it took, just a couple of hours of focusing on work, and I felt like a different person, completely empowered. I was conducting business; of course, not at the level accustomed to me. I wasn't anywhere near full strength in terms of what I normally did on my job. However, I was still needed beyond the walls of my home.

Throughout the day, I hadn't had time to give much thought to my neck, or the surgery, or to what was going on with me now. For just a part of the day, I was normal. Even if I couldn't see a thing.

CHAPTER 13

Even with all that Siri could do for me, Siri couldn't help with the fact that I was still very much limited physically. The strain of keeping my head down was so taxing, and no matter what I tried, it was hard to find a comfortable position. I couldn't spend long hours in the chair—at most, I could sit there for about an hour and "watch" TV. Sometimes I'd sit, then lay on the sofa. However, the place that brought me the most relief from the pressure on my neck was laying in my bed.

In that first week, I found myself in bed a lot. For someone who had been so active and not at all used to being confined to home, this was different for me. I used that time, though, not only to rest but to reflect. There were still so many questions in my head.

I just wanted the days to pass by faster, not only for me but for Tina, too. As tough as all of this was on me, my surgery and recovery were tough on my wife as well. This was a lot for Tina to handle. There was so much to do with taking care of me: getting me back and forth to the doctor, making sure

I had my eye drops four times a day on time, helping me do everything from eating to getting dressed. She had to do all of that while continuing to work full time as well.

Tina's company had given her the ability to work from home, but her responsibilities remained. She held a demanding position in a Fortune 100 company; from managing projects to attending meetings and still working with her staff, there was a lot on her plate.

Taking care of me and maintaining her job was a huge undertaking, but Tina did it without complaint and concern. Today, there is one thing that I know for sure—I would have never gotten through all of this without her.

Day by day, the bubble in my eye continued to dissolve, giving me a more subtle glimpse into the world. If I held my head in a certain position, I could see the numbers or apps on my phone, and soon I could see my feet. My vision was still quite blurry. It still felt as if I was looking through purple Kool-Aid, but slowly, my vision was coming back; this felt like progress to me.

Spending so much time laying down often made it difficult to sleep at night, but I used that time (sometimes long after midnight) constructively. I'd lay there and pray, meditate or listen to spiritual and motivational audiobooks.

The hours I spent listening helped to not only put me in a very peaceful state, but those books kept me there. As we approached the end of my first week, I could recognize and give thanks for all I'd achieved to this point. The worst was behind me. I had to continue to settle in and keep doing my part.

That was my frame of mind as Sunday came and Tina and I got ready for my next doctor's appointment on Monday. I was excited, anxious to get back to see Dr. Chang and get another positive report of my progress.

However, the probability of hearing good news from Dr. Chang wasn't the only reason for my excitement. The doctor's appointment gave us an opportunity to break up the monotony of being in the apartment. Both Tina and I needed that fresh air.

Sunday night, we prepared for the early morning appointment by laying out all of my clothes and everything else I'd need for the trip. This time was a little different from last week's appointment. Tina had to help me with everything before, but now, I could do a little more on my own with my sight returning just a bit. I was cautious in my movements, though.

Filled with anxiety, I didn't rest well the night before. We were both anxious, so once the sun rose, we were ready to go, wanting to get a bit ahead of the Midtown morning rush hour traffic. Tina and I were out of our apartment by seven, taking that same path down the hallway to the garage. She held onto me on one side, and on the other side, I slid my hand against the wall, once again counting my steps along the way.

Even though I was close to a week into this, I still moved with caution, especially since we were outside of our apartment. There were always things that could trip me up—a dip in the carpet, or something on the ground.

The little excitement I had that hadn't been taken away by my anxiety left me once I slid into the car. I was smacked right in the face (or should I say the neck) with the pain. The pressure was steady, a throbbing that stayed for the entire hour that it took us to travel from New Jersey to the east side of Manhattan. The pain made me irritable. So instead of talking, I focused on the good report I hoped to hear from Dr. Chang.

It was a relief to make it to the doctor's office finally, but once we parked in the garage, I was faced with the same set of challenges from our last appointment: I felt vulnerable and inadequate. Like before, the attendants were pleasant as they greeted us, but I imagined what they thought when they saw me: this tall, built guy completely dependent on his petite wife. What I was going through now reminded me of the times when I'd watch a blind person or anyone dependent on someone else. There was always sorrow in my heart and now, I questioned if everyone was feeling sorry for me. All of it was a blow to my ego.

My self-consciousness didn't diminish when I walked into Dr. Chang's office. Of course, his receptionist had greeted hundreds of people like me, but still, the entire experience was humbling.

After Tina signed us in, she led me to a chair next to the wall, and the moment I sat down, I rubbed my aching neck.

Tina asked, "Are you okay?"

Her question was always the same, but so was her sentiment. She really wanted to know, to make sure that I was good at all times.

"I'm okay, but my trapezoid muscles."

She didn't say anything, although I knew if she thought there was something she could say or do to take that pain away from me, she would have.

As we waited to be called back to Dr. Chang's office, I tried to take my focus away from the literal pain in my neck to what was important. I prayed and said my affirmations, focusing on everything being okay with my retina.

We were finally called by one of Dr. Chang's assistants. The pleasant young woman spoke in a tone that made me relax right away. As she moved us back to the examination room, I could tell she'd done this a million times.

Once I sat in the examination chair, she asked, "How are you doing?"

"Okay."

"Are you taking the eye drops?"

"Every day and on time. My wife makes sure of it."

I waited as patiently as I could as she took my vitals— checking the pressure in my eye, then she had me read the eye chart before she prepped me for the doctor.

"Okay, Dr. Chang will be right with you."

As Tina and I sat and waited, once again I took myself back to my prayers and affirmations, keeping my thoughts there and not on my discomfort. It didn't take long for Dr. Chang to come into the room; he never kept me waiting.

"How are you doing, Steve?"

"I'm okay." I then answered his questions about taking the eye drops and keeping my head down. "I'm doing all of that, Dr. Chang, but my neck is really aching."

"I know," he said, and I could hear the empathy in his voice. "But there's not much you can do about that. Are you using all of the equipment?"

"I am. The chair is not as comfortable as I'd hoped it would be, but I'm using everything."

"Okay, let me take a look at your eye." He had me lean forward and rest my chin on the machine that was connected to the examination chair. First, he spread my eyelids apart, and then he shone the light into my eye. The light wasn't as piercing as the coal miner's light, and I was glad about that.

"Okay," Dr. Chang said, "Look up and then down." After I followed his instructions, he said, "Now to the left…now to the right."

A couple of minutes later, he turned off the light and rolled his stool over to the desk where he jotted down a few notes. Once he completed that, he stood, then reclined my chair. I knew what that meant—it was time for the coal miner's light and the magnifying glass.

As much as I always hated this part of the exam, it wasn't as intense because of the gas bubble. The purplish haze absorbed some of the brightness.

Still, it was a relief when he turned off the light and said, "Everything looks good."

"What about the bubble? Is everything fine?"

"Yes. The bubble will continue to dissolve. Just continue to keep your head down and sleep correctly. Stay on your right side. But all in all, everything looks good. You're doing fine."

Dr. Chang's words gave me a massive feeling of relief. This was what I'd hoped to hear. We set another appointment for Friday. After that, Tina and I headed home to begin the second week of this journey.

CHAPTER 14

My life became a series of routines. I continued to spend a lot of time laying down because that was the best way for me to handle the pain of the pressure on my neck since the chair didn't give me much relief.

I'd lay down and listen to Sports Center to catch up on what was happening in the world of sports, or The Wendy Williams Show to hear what was going on in the world of pop culture. There were times when I'd turn to the news stations to know what was going on in the world of politics. Often, listening to one of the three, I would doze off, which, again, made it difficult to sleep through the night.

When I was awake, though, Tina and I had our routine around the apartment. My wife had it all down to a science, from preparing my meals or ordering food from Good Eats, to making sure I had my eye drops right on schedule and anything else I needed. She was always there to meet any of my needs, by my side all the time, even as she held down her nine-to-five.

I also had my work routine. Even though I wasn't a work-at-home kind of guy, I had to get into work mode. Everyone at the office was understanding of my situation, but I still didn't want any kind of lapse in production.

So around nine-thirty every morning, I'd make my first call of the day to my sales support team to see how many deals had come in the day before. Then, I reviewed all the appointments that were set for that day. Throughout the next hours, I spoke with the reps in the field to see if any of them needed my assistance in closing their deals. Since we were coming up to the end of the month, I wanted to finish strong.

I worked until the close of business, reserving the evenings for speaking with my family and friends. I spoke to Smitty and my brother every day, discussing my progress and how I was feeling. Talking to them was a great escape; I could lay my burdens on their shoulders rather than on Tina's.

My brother always ended our conversation by telling me he'd make a strong Dua (a prayer in the Islamic faith) for my recovery. There was such a deep sincerity in his tone when he said those words that always touched my spirit and comforted me.

Smitty's serene and soothing tone always put me at ease, no matter what I told him. Talking to him, I felt like the kid whose father was letting him know everything was going to be all right.

Another person who I called often was Pico. I'd known him for more than nineteen years in the fellowship. For much of his adult life, Pico had been over three hundred pounds and had gotten to where just breathing and walking were difficult.

"Steven, I've got to do something about my weight," he'd told me. "I've got to be healthier because I want to be around for my grandson."

Pico and I had similar ideologies. He wanted to get healthier for his grandson so he wouldn't be a burden on his family, and I felt the same way. I wanted to have my sight to see my granddaughter grow up and to not be a burden on Tina and my children.

Pico told me, "I'm going to have gastric sleeve surgery."

I encouraged him to do that. Just a few days after my surgery, he had his and we went through the healing process together. After his surgery, he couldn't eat much, and his weight loss was a long, slow process with a lot of challenges. I understood what he was going through, so we talked often about our emotional struggles. Our conversations were constantly positive because they always ended with us remembering our faith and encouraging each other.

The routine that was the most important and the one that made the most difference was what I did daily in my spiritual life. I had always been a spiritual person, always having a sense of a Higher Power. But like many, my faith didn't develop until I had to go through a few of life's adversities and had no choice but to call on this Higher Power more often.

There were so many things that drew me closer to God: all the eye surgeries I had to go through as a child and a teen, having once been addicted to drugs and my recovery from that, then finally, the death of my mother. Coming through all of those very tough situations allowed me to see there was a Power greater than myself that was within me. I had not just survived these experiences, I'd grown through them and had become a better man because of each situation. That could only have happened because of God, my Higher Power.

So like I've said, this was a time of my life filled with spirituality. In the morning, I'd pray, meditate, and "read" Joel Osteen's I Declare: 31 Promises to Speak Over Your Life. It was a book filled with affirmations that I would listen to and then I began to say my own affirmations:

"Thank you, God, that my family is safe."

"Thank you, God, that my eye is healing."

"Thank you, God, that my vision is 20/20 and my eye is healed."

I knew the words I spoke over myself and my life would play a huge role in my healing, so I continuously spoke positivity over my situation and family.

Two of my favorite books to listen to were Conversations with God: An Uncommon Dialogue and As a Man Thinketh. These books really helped to strengthen my spiritual awareness. Conversations with God: An Uncommon Dialogue helped me to realize that God wasn't some blinding light from the sky with the voice of James Earl Jones, but a real Power that lived within me. As a Man Thinketh helped me to understand how to activate that power through my thinking, by consciously focusing on the positive, visualizing positive outcomes of situations, and eliminating negative words from my vocabulary as much as possible.

My healing became a time of relying on my faith and my family. With God and everyone else, I truly believed it was all going to come together for me.

--๑~๑)

Each day the bubble dissolved a little more, and I could maneuver a bit more by myself. I was still nowhere near being independent because I had to keep my head down and I was still looking through a glass of grape Kool-Aid. However, the little bit of light made me less dependent on Tina. By tilting my head, I could see the furniture so I could move around by counting steps and using the wall. Every day felt like progress.

It was still tough, though. Even with my routines, I was developing a serious case of cabin fever. It was frustrating that there was nothing I could do about that because leaving our apartment was not an option.

So once again, when my appointment with Dr. Chang rolled around on the 31st, I was excited. We were going out. Waking up that morning, I felt as if I were going on an adventure, especially since I felt more independent than last week.

As the journey began, it was the same: the discomfort in my neck was the same, my self-consciousness was the same, and the assistant who prepped me for Dr. Chang was the same, though there was one thing different with the prep. When I took the eye test and read the chart, the assistant told me that my vision was 20/70 which was a really good sign that all was going well.

When Dr. Chang asked me all the questions he'd asked before—how I was doing, was I taking the drops on time—I told him everything was good, though I still had the pain in my neck.

However, there was a little shift in the conversation. "I see a tiny bit of fluid," the doctor said as he studied my eye, "but it's nothing to worry about. That should go away."

There was not a bit of concern in Dr. Chang's voice, so since he wasn't concerned, I wasn't either.

Then he gave me the best news of all. "After tomorrow, you won't have to keep your head down anymore. Now some of the bubble will still be there, but it will dissolve completely, eventually."

My first thought when I heard his words was that my shoulder and neck muscles would really appreciate that.

On the ride home, I didn't feel my usual agitation. Even though I had my head down, I was counting the hours to when I could look up. This major part of my healing was almost over.

As Tina drove, I tilted my head and checked out the license plates of the cars in front of me. I could see most of them, which to me just added to the good news of the day. First, I had 20/70 vision and after tonight, I'd no longer have to keep my head down. Not only was the surgery a success, but the two weeks of healing had gone well, too. I couldn't go back to work yet because my eye needed to heal some more. But now, I'd be more functional.

I could hold my head up. It was time to exhale.

CHAPTER 15

Tina and I lived in a condo complex with a mall that had a grocery store and other retail businesses on the lower level. Once I could lift my head, I decided to go downstairs. I didn't need anything; I just loved the fact that I could venture out a little bit on my own.

As I stepped into the hallway, I felt nervous, and for the first time since I had this idea, I thought of everything that could happen to me. I hoped I didn't see anyone I knew; I felt like I could handle anything except for someone asking me a lot of questions. I wasn't ready for that.

I moved carefully and cautiously, not quite feeling comfortable. But I made it—I took the elevator, went to the grocery store, purchased a bottle of water, and then returned to our apartment. I'd done that all without Tina, and that was a major accomplishment for me.

Every day I saw more and more progress. As I watched television (and yes, I was really watching it now), I'd follow the news-ticker that scrolled on the bottom of the screen if I was watching the news. As I watched a basketball game, I studied to make sure I could see the scores. On both counts, I was successful.

There was no doubt that each day I was getting better, so after a few weeks went by, I was ready to do something big.

"Let's go to the movies," I told Tina.

"Are you sure?"

I nodded. I was very sure. I was ready to do something that made me feel as if I was getting a piece of my life back. Of course, Tina had to drive, but we went to see Straight Outta Compton. I was excited as we sat in the theatre with popcorn in our hands. My life was coming back.

However, as the movie played on, my eyesight seemed a little off. I couldn't see solid images. The images I could see were spotty, as if there were gray holes in everything. After a while, though, I pushed that thought aside. This was my first time out and I was sitting in a dark room with a large projection screen. There was nothing wrong.

After the success of the movie, I took an even bigger step. In the fellowship, we held a men's meeting every Saturday morning. I loved this NA meeting because it gave men a chance to share sensitive issues they might not share if women were present. Since I didn't have to hold my head down anymore, I wanted to go.

I told Tina about my plans, but I added that I didn't want her to take me. A buddy of mine who was part of the fellowship lived in Englewood, New Jersey, which was close to where we lived. I told her I would call Rick to see if I could catch a ride with him.

When I spoke to him on the phone, Rick said, "Sure, I'll pick you up. I'm just going to be staying in the city after the meeting, so you'll have to catch a ride back with someone else."

"That's cool," I told him.

I hung up from Rick and called my sponsor, Dwight, to arrange for him to bring me back home. He agreed. We hadn't seen each other in a while and the ride would give us a chance to catch up.

This was so exciting. Not only was I leaving the apartment, but I was going to a meeting by myself…well, I wouldn't exactly be by myself, but Tina wouldn't have to take me.

While I was filled with excitement, a bit of anxiety tried to slip in, too. Of course, it was because of all the questions I put in my head: Could I really do this without Tina? Would it be safe?

Questions were in my head, but I wasn't going to let any of that stop me. I had to do this for my own empowerment.

On Saturday morning, Tina walked me down to Boulevard East, where we waited for Rick. I was filled with all kinds of emotions in the five minutes (that felt like two hours) it took for Rick to arrive. When he pulled up, my emotions spilled over. Rick was a representation of the fellowship to me, the place where, over these nineteen years, I'd been able to go to find hope and comfort, no matter what was going on in my life.

While Rick drove, we chatted about my experience with the surgery and I told him about how the spiritual principles of the fellowship were helping to get me through.

As what had become my custom, I paid attention to the license plates on the passing cars, just as a way to check my vision. But as we rode over the George Washington Bridge, my vision seemed off a bit. It seemed a bit dark and spotty. Just like the night before, though, I attributed that to just my excitement about returning to a normal part of my life.

About thirty-five minutes later, we arrived at the meeting in the Soundview section of the Bronx. I had to calm myself down from all that I was feeling—I was that excited. I couldn't wait to get into the meeting.

Inside, I greeted Smitty, who was so glad to see me since we'd only talked on the phone. From there, the greetings continued, but very quickly I noticed that as people came up to greet and hug me, I couldn't see them very well. I had to keep apologizing for not recognizing the men and explaining that I'd just had eye surgery.

Like the night before in the theatre and the car, the room was dark, spotty and images were not solid. Once again, I made an excuse for what I was seeing. I just needed to adjust to the lighting. After all, it had been a while since I'd been in a room like this, and after surgery, my eyes probably needed time to adjust when I went from natural sunlight to indoor lighting. There was always an adjustment with the retina—at least, that was how I was explaining it to myself.

When too many minutes passed and my eyes still didn't adjust, an uneasy feeling overcame me. Once the meeting began, I sat next to Smitty, but I had a hard time focusing. I kept searching the room, trying to make out the people and the furniture, but nothing was right. As I looked all around the room, the people who had always given me so much hope were nothing more than shadowy figures.

Today was supposed to be another triumphant step in my healing process, but it quickly became an hour and thirty minutes of horror.

At the end of the meeting, I said to Dwight, "Listen, I need to call Tina. Something's going on with my eye."

"Okay," he said, in his usual mild-mannered way.

I wanted Tina to come and pick me up. There was nothing she could do, but honestly, I just felt emotionally safer with her.

Tina was out with our daughter, Rachel, when I called and asked her to pick me up from the meeting.

"Is everything okay? I thought Dwight was bringing you home," she said, and I knew her questions were only because she and Rachel were out running errands.

"He has an emergency," I said, feeling like it was too much to explain over the phone. I didn't want her to panic.

That was all I had to say to my wife. Tina said, "Oh, okay," and she left our daughter shopping and came straight to me. We made plans for her to meet me on 181st Street and Broadway, at the entrance to the George Washington Bridge. Dwight drove me over there and when we arrived, I thanked him, told him I'd see him soon, then got into the car with Tina.

I didn't say anything after I greeted her and as we rode home, I checked out the license plates of the cars around me. I couldn't read any of them. The darkness and the spottiness continued.

Panic really rose in me, but I said nothing to Tina. I didn't want to alarm her until I could think about this some more and figure this out. Keeping this from Tina wasn't going to be easy; it was difficult to hide anything from my wife.

The moment we stepped into our apartment, she asked, "What's wrong? Why are you so quiet?"

At first, I told her, "Nothing," because I wanted to take the time to see if anything would change now that we were home. But as I sat on the sofa, like everything else, our apartment looked darker than usual.

"Well, if you're good now, I'm going to go back and pick up Rachel."

"I'm good," I said, pretending everything was okay until she walked out the door.

Once she was gone, I turned on the television, prepared to give myself another test. Just like with the license plates, I couldn't make out the wording on the news ticker at the bottom of the screen as I "tried" to watch the news the way I'd been doing. That was when I knew for sure that something was really wrong, and I didn't want to waste any more time or take any kind of chances.

Tina hadn't been gone too long when I called her again. "Something's wrong." As calmly as I could, I explained to her the changes in my vision.

For the second time that day, she left Rachel. As soon as she walked through the door, she said, "I'm calling the doctor." I wondered if she thought this was a false alarm, but I was her baby; she wasn't going to take any chances.

We called Dr. Chang's office, not expecting to get him, of course, since this was the weekend. I knew we'd get an operator who would connect us to the doctor on call.

When Tina got through to the answering service, she said, "My husband is a patient of Dr. Chang and he had surgery recently."

As Tina explained, I really hoped it would be Dr. Chang who would call me back. About ten minutes after Tina hung up, the phone rang, but it wasn't my doctor; a resident was on the other end. I explained to the doctor what was going on—how everything seemed so dark, how nothing was in focus.

"All right," he said when I finished. "I think you should get to the hospital so I can examine you right away."

When I hung up, Tina and I just looked at each other. I didn't want to worry, but I knew this was a new part of my journey.

The ride to Lennox Hill Hospital in Manhattan was somber, to say the least. Tina and I sat in an eerie silence all the way there. I was trying to go within myself to find a safe space so I'd be ready for what was to come. I think Tina's silence was her strength. She was going to be strong and show no signs of panic.

In front of the hospital, Tina pulled up to the curb. "I'm going to take you inside and then I'll park the car."

It was a Saturday, so Lennox Hill hospital wasn't as active as it was on any weekday; it was rather empty. In fact, in the lobby where I had to wait, only one other gentleman was sitting there. We checked in with the person at the front desk, then made our way to the seating area. Tina asked me if I was okay.

After just a few moments, the other man and I started talking. We discovered that we were waiting to see the same doctor, though his situation wasn't an emergency. He was getting a post-op examination.

We chatted, sharing our experiences and talking about our professions. About fifteen minutes later, Tina came in and I introduced her to the man who had helped me pass the time.

After the gentleman was called upstairs, Tina and I just sat there and chatted awkwardly, which was strange for us. Finally, it was a relief to be called up to the doctor. When we exited the elevator, the hallway was dark. At first, it was a bit startling until I realized the hospital had turned off the overhead lights. There was only light coming from two examination rooms.

We walked in the direction of the voices we heard. When we were a few feet from the door, the doctor came out, walking beside an elderly woman. As he passed us, he nodded and said, "I'll be right with you." He motioned for us to go into the examination room.

From his voice, I recognized him to be the doctor I'd spoken with and he was as young as I thought, probably somewhere in his late twenties to early thirties.

He returned to the examination room just a few minutes later. "Okay, so what's going on?"

Even though Tina and I had just told him, I repeated what I'd explained on the phone.

"Okay," he said when I finished, "let's take your vision first."

I turned to the eye chart and what I saw stunned me. Or rather, what I should say is what I couldn't see shocked me. I could hardly read the big "E" on the chart. That big "E" was equivalent to 20/200 vision!

It was blurry and I definitely couldn't see any of the letters beneath it. Just a few days before, I read the letters on the 20/70 line on the chart.

After the eye test, the doctor put dilating drops in my eye, then checked the pressure.

"We'll wait ten minutes for your eyes to completely dilate. I'll be right back."

A few moments later, I heard him in the next examination room speaking with the gentleman I'd met in the lobby.

Tina and I sat in silence and I could only imagine her thoughts. I was so worried—my vision had been reduced to 20/200.

When the doctor returned to me, it was time for the dreaded coal miner's light so he could look at my retina. Having to lay back and open my eye, looking left, looking right, looking up and down—it was all too familiar.

The doctor clicked off the light, then looked at me. "I'm going to call Dr. Chang."

For a moment, I waited for him to tell me something more. Certainly, he was going to tell me why he was calling Dr. Chang. When he didn't say anything else, I asked, "What's wrong with my eye?"

"Let me speak to Dr. Chang and then I'll explain everything to you."

I was surprised when he didn't leave the room and called Dr. Chang right there in front of Tina and me. My wife was silent, but I could feel that she was on the edge of panic—just like I was.

As the doctor spoke to Dr. Chang, he used medical terms I didn't understand. However, there was one part of the conversation that was very clear.

"His vision is now 20/200."

Suddenly, the doctor was quiet as Dr. Chang now did all the talking.

All the young doctor kept saying was, "Uh-huh, uh-huh, okay, okay."

Finally, he clicked off his cell phone and turned to me. "Dr. Chang wants us to schedule surgery for you."

"Okay," I said, trying to keep my composure.

The doctor added, "We're scheduling the surgery for tomorrow."

"Tomorrow," I said, incredulously.

He nodded.

That meant there was a big problem. Because not only was tomorrow a Sunday, which had to make the surgery all the more serious, but tomorrow was also Father's Day. Who would schedule surgery for Father's Day unless it was an absolute emergency?

CHAPTER 16

Time slowed and I felt numb. I was walking through a fog as the doctor explained it all to me.

"You have a lot of leaking in the retina," he said. "We have to get you into surgery because the leakage is at the point where it can do permanent damage."

I couldn't believe this was happening. I had made it through the two weeks of holding my head down. I'd done everything I was supposed to do. Yet, I was in danger of permanent damage?

"So we're going to get you into surgery tomorrow morning. Early, at seven."

"Wow, it must be serious," I said.

The doctor only nodded.

For the first time, I didn't have any more questions or anything else to say. How could I when I was struggling to process what I'd just been told?

As Tina and I walked out of the hospital, we didn't say a word to each other. The silence screamed on the ride home. I didn't know what Tina was feeling, but she seemed to be cool and calm and I was happy about that. I didn't want her to be worried.

At home, the silence between us continued, but it didn't bother me. I needed the quiet to process this day, and I guessed Tina was giving me the space to handle this in my own way.

While I needed the space, I also needed to process this by talking it through. So, I turned to Smitty and my brother. I called Smitty first and after I explained the situation to him, he told me in that calm, soothing voice of his, that God had a plan for my life and everything was already worked out. We talked for about twenty minutes and the entire time, Smitty encouraged me. I hung up feeling much better than before I called.

Next, when I spoke to my brother, his words were so similar to Smitty's. Only, of course, he talked about Allah instead of God.

After those two calls, I was in a better place, but when I lay down to rest that night, sleep didn't come easy. Competing thoughts volleyed through my head, keeping me awake until I finally rolled out of the bed and got on my knees. I took my concerns to God. I prayed about the surgery and thanked God for His guidance with the doctor and His healing power over me.

When I got back in bed, I rested. I can't say I slept much, but that was fine. After my prayers, I was filled with peace and serenity.

As we rode to the hospital early on Sunday morning, it was still amazing that we were doing this today. Although

Tina's presence was as comforting to me as it always was, we didn't try to break the silence between us, knowing we each had to process our own feelings.

I thought back to some of the things the doctor had said yesterday: "Using a laser, we'll go in, find the portion that is leaking, and close the hole."

It seemed like a simple process, but it was so much more. Something had gone wrong. Yes, it could be fixed, but it was a problem, nonetheless.

When we got to the hospital, everything was different from all the surgeries I'd had in the past. First, Tina and I had to wait in the lobby for a while before the young doctor from the day before came and took us to another building to be registered. Since surgeries weren't usually scheduled for Sundays, everything was done right in the operating room. I changed into my gown and washed my eye in the operating room's bathroom.

Two nurses assisted me as I was moved to the operating table, and a junior anesthesiologist prepared the IV for my hand. Once that was done, Dr. Chang came into the operating room.

"How are you doing, Steve?"

"Well, I didn't expect to be here today."

He nodded.

I said, "Happy Father's Day. This must have been serious for you to schedule the surgery so suddenly."

"It is, but it can be fixed." Then Dr. Chang explained what the doctor had told me yesterday. "And once we fix the hole, we'll reinsert another bubble to stabilize the retina."

"Okay." I took a deep breath. I was ready.

But then the doctor added, "We can't start yet, Steve. We weren't able to get in touch with an anesthesiologist, but we've contacted the head of anesthesiology and he'll be here. He has to drive into the city, so we have to give him a little time."

I had been doing well, but this news made my anxiety rise. Of course, they were having a difficult time finding someone, especially on this Sunday.

Waiting for the anesthesiologist was agonizing. All I wanted to do was start so this could end. We waited about ninety minutes before the head of anesthesiology rushed into the operating room.

"I'm so sorry," he said, apologizing to everyone.

I appreciated his apology, but it certainly wasn't his fault that he wasn't here on time for emergency surgery on Father's Day. I was just glad he was finally here.

"Okay, let's get this started," Dr. Chang said. Like before, he put a mark on my forehead right above my left eye, which gave me a moment of comic relief. This amused me because we were about to do this very specialized surgery and this mark on my forehead seemed so pedestrian.

I thought I was going to have local anesthesia like the first time, but this time, Dr. Chang had me completely unconscious. I had no idea how long I'd been out, but I woke up in the operating room, feeling groggy with gauze over my eye.

The first voice I heard was the doctor from the day before. "Steve, Dr. Chang will be coming back in here to speak with you shortly."

It didn't seem like even a minute passed before Dr. Chang came back into the operating room.

"It went well, Steve. I'm sorry we had to wait so long for the anesthesiologist." Then he gave me instructions for the rest of the day and tomorrow.

Shortly after, the nurses let Tina into the operating room, and like always, she asked, "How are you feeling?"

"Fine," I told her, already feeling a little better because her voice gave me comfort.

"Stephanee is going to meet us here. She planned to surprise you for Father's Day."

I nodded. At least that part of Father's Day would be great. Stephanee was our youngest and she'd been away at college. I was sure when she put together this plan, she didn't expect to surprise me here at the hospital.

"Mr. King." My head turned to the sound of the nurse's voice. "How are you feeling?"

I nodded. "Fine."

Everything about today was different. I was prepped in the operating room and now, it seemed my recovery and discharge were going to happen in here as well. The nurse took my temperature and blood pressure.

"Do you want some juice or crackers?"

"No."

"Well, relax for a little while. I'll be back."

Even though Tina was with me, I closed my eyes, still feeling groggy. About thirty minutes later the nurse returned and once again took my temperature and blood pressure. She then told me it was fine for me to get dressed.

Like always, Tina assisted me. She helped me into the bathroom, then helped me get dressed, being extra cautious and attentive. Her voice kept me sane and comforted.

Once I was ready, we thanked the medical staff and one of the nurses rolled me down to the lobby where Tina and I waited for my daughter to arrive.

I was both excited and disappointed as I waited for Stephanee. I was excited that I was going to have my daughter in my company, but so frustrated that she would see me in such a vulnerable state. I wondered how she would react because I'd always been her rock and her protector. She had never seen me this way. When my daughter walked through the revolving door, though, my spirit was lifted. I was excited that she was there.

"Hey, Dad," she said as she hugged me.

I felt so comforted by her embrace. When she stepped back, I listened attentively for some sign of what she was feeling.

"Are you okay?"

"Of course I am, baby girl." And then, hoping to lighten the mood and her concern, I said, "I'm happy to see you, well, not literally, but you know what I mean."

She gave me that familiar laugh, which was always her response whenever I told a corny dad joke.

Tina said, "Okay, I'm going to get the car from the parking lot."

When she left us alone, I realized the joke hadn't been enough. Even though I'd tried, I still felt awkward and uncomfortable, wondering what my daughter was thinking.

While I was concerned about her, I didn't want her to be concerned about me. So I initiated some pointless conversation, and she obliged with pointless responses.

But after a few minutes of chatter about nothing, Stephanee whispered, "Are you okay?"

"Of course I am," I said confidently. "This surgery was minor. There's nothing to worry about."

When Tina finally pulled up in front of the hospital, Stephanee helped me to the car, and my daughter was as careful with me as Tina. Once I settled inside, I had to fight the thoughts in my head: how I was right back at the beginning, how I had to, once again, keep my head down. Of course, I was grateful the leakage had been caught in time, but the thought of starting over was depressing.

I was exhausted by all of this, but I didn't want my wife and daughter to see that, so once again, I initiated the conversation and kept the mood light. There was hardly any traffic, it was Father's Day, so we were home within twenty minutes.

I felt nothing but relief when we walked into our apartment. The first thing I did was have Tina help me change into pajamas. Then, all I wanted to do was lay down on the sofa. This time I wasn't only trying to ease the pain in my neck; I needed to rest and recover from all the stress of the day. What I'd been through was a lot physically—we had to get up so early; it was a lot emotionally—going through this once again was tough.

"Is there anything you need, Dad?"

"No, I'm good." I was really happy to see Stephanee, but I was really struggling with my daughter seeing me this way.

I was grateful when Stephanee turned her attention to her phone. Sitting across from me on the sectional, I heard videos playing. I imagined she was on her social media accounts. Tina was on the phone as well, answering the barrage of calls from friends and family who wanted an update on what happened today.

Laying on the sofa with my eyes closed while everyone in my family was concerned about me was not the way I thought we'd be spending Father's Day, but I reminded myself to remain thankful.

We were home for a couple of hours when Tina jumped up suddenly. "I'm going out," she said.

I didn't ask where she was going. I figured she was running to the store. Once she left, I stayed resting on the sofa, but I couldn't sleep. I tried listening to the television, but I couldn't really hear it through the question I kept asking myself: How had this happened?

After a while, I sat up. Tired of being in the same position, I asked Stephanee to accompany me to the kitchen. I wasn't very hungry, but I needed a glass of water.

The cup was in my hand when I heard the front door open and then I heard Tina's voice.

"Steve, I have a surprise for you."

In the seconds before I turned around, I guessed that I'd been right. Tina had gone to the store, probably to get a Father's Day cake to cheer me up.

Then, all of a sudden, this little angelic voice rang out. "Hi, Grandpa." The sweet voice of my three-year-old granddaughter floated up to my ears.

All the frustration stored inside of me from everything that happened yesterday and today was stripped away, and I was overwhelmed with joy. I couldn't see Parker, but hearing her was enough.

When I turned to Parker, she said, "What happened to your eye, Grandpa?"

"Well, Grandpa hurt his eye, and the doctor had to fix it."

"How did you hurt your eye?" Her tone filled with curiosity.

"It was an accident."

"An accident?"

"Yes, baby, an accident."

I knew that if I didn't change the subject, she was going to keep questioning me. So, I said, "Can you help me get back to the couch?"

She grabbed my hand. "Okay, Grandpa. I'll help you." As carefully as she could, she led me out of the kitchen and over to the sofa. Once I sat down, she asked, "Are you okay?" In her little sweet voice, I heard all of her concern.

"Yes, I'm fine, baby." I lifted her onto my lap and hugged her. She was such a bright spot in the middle of all of this darkness.

Our moment together lasted just a minute as her attention shifted. She wiggled her way out of my hug and off of my lap before she ran over to Tina.

"Gigi, can I play with my toys?"

Not long after that, my son and my granddaughter's mother arrived with a bunch of food. In just moments, the apartment was transformed into a festive gathering, with lots of hugs and laughter and plenty of chatter.

As I sat in the middle of all of this joy, I felt so many emotions. Who knew the weekend would end with good food, good conversation, just a good time?

For this time, I pushed aside all the physical reminders of my state. Yes, my head was down, yes, I couldn't see right now, but I was going to bask in these moments. My family was here to celebrate me. After all, it was Father's Day.

CHAPTER 17

I went to sleep feeling quite good. My family held me down for Father's Day. However, then Monday came. Tina and I had to pick right back up with everything that we thought was almost over. With my head down again (though it wasn't as bad since this time I knew what to expect), I felt as if my independence had been snatched from me.

Inside the car, as we made our way to Dr. Chang's office, I was back to feeling vulnerable and self-conscious. It was déjà vu as we waited for Dr. Chang and then being led back to the examination room. When Dr. Chang walked in, I heard sincere compassion for me in his words and his tone.

Dr. Chang and I went through the normal greetings and questions before he examined me. At the end, he said, "Okay, Steve, everything looks good, but this time, we're going to monitor you a bit more."

He suggested I continue to come to him on Mondays, but I should see another doctor so only a few days would pass between each examination.

"I could see Dr. Freilich," I said.

"Yes, that would work." Dr. Chang nodded. "I'll call and update him on your condition."

I left that appointment with gratitude and hope. Everything hadn't moved forward as we planned, but I would be fine. I believed that.

Once we were back home, I contacted my job. This call was going to be sobering. I had expected to call today to inform the partners of the firm that I'd be returning to work soon. Now, I had to tell him that I wouldn't be back for a while.

Alex picked up the phone and after exchanging pleasantries, I went straight to the truth. "I had to have another surgery."

It was at that moment when the fog-like dream state I felt like I'd been in disappeared. I was facing the complete reality of what this second surgery meant. I would not be going back to work for at least another month.

There was an awkward pause and then he said, "Okay, Steve. You have to do what you need to do to get better." After another pause, he asked, "How do you feel?"

"Fine, I just hate starting over, but I'll be fine. And I'm keeping up with my team."

When I hung up, I was even more frustrated than I was before I called. I was back to ground zero, but I wasn't alone. Tina was right there with me. She was back to totally taking care of me while balancing her demanding work schedule. It was frustrating for both of us, but all we could do was make it through.

As the days passed, I was filled with much more paranoia than before. However, to me, that wasn't a bad thing. If I had waited even one more day before I contacted Dr. Chang on Saturday, this situation would have turned out totally different.

So this time I looked out for everything. Like before, for the first couple of days, I couldn't see anything. Then, as the bubble began to dissolve, I began to see a bit of light. However, my eye was filled with floaters and flashers that looked like black eels swooshing around in an aquarium.

My paranoia had me calling the doctor with any little change in my vision. If the flash of light looked different, I called. If the shape of the floaters changed, I called. I was cautious and careful. This second surgery changed all of my plans, and I wasn't going to let it happen again.

I felt strange as I prepared for my first appointment after the surgery with Dr. Freilich. I felt as if I had let him down in some way. When I met with him just a few days after seeing Dr. Chang, I felt a shift in his energy, too. He was so sympathetic and compassionate, I wondered if he thought he'd let me down.

After a few minutes of being together, and my answering his questions, we both settled in. He examined me, and then Dr. Freilich confirmed what Dr. Chang had told me: "There is no fault to place in this situation. Your eye has been a volatile situation going all the way back to Dr. Chess."

I nodded as I remembered the doctor who'd referred to my eye as a land mine.

"These are the risks," Dr. Freilich said. "The good news is that it was caught in time and I believe from this point, you'll be okay. This is a good idea for you to see both Dr. Chang and me. We'll keep a closer eye on you."

The visit with Dr. Freilich raised my confidence. I was working with two of the best doctors. There was nothing more that I could ask for. God had given me the best, and that was where I was going to keep my focus.

CHAPTER 18

The good thing about the second surgery was that it really forced me to meditate and pray even more diligently. Every morning I got out of bed, usually before Tina awakened, and felt my way into the living room. I was a pro now. I knew the number of steps from the bedroom into the living room and my other senses kicked in, taking over for my sight. I was keenly aware of everything: every piece of furniture, every dip in the floor. All of that helped me to navigate around our apartment.

One of the beautiful things about our place was that every window faced east overlooking the Hudson River, giving us a clear, unobstructed view of Manhattan and its skyline. Inside the living room, I would sit in the chair, facing the window. Of course, I couldn't see the view, but I felt it. From there I would meditate, pray, and reflect on my blessings. I felt empowered in these early morning moments, determined not to allow this setback to defeat me. I chose not to let any kind of depression overcome me; depression couldn't hit a moving target and I was going to keep it moving.

I began to look at this second surgery as a victory; I'd been saved from permanent blindness, and this state I was in now was not going to be my destiny. This too would pass. Even though I had to go through this, I was going to get through it. I was going to fight.

Joel Osteen's I Declare had already been a staple in my spiritual routine, but now I ramped that up a notch. Each day I'd listen to the daily declaration. At the end of the book is a long summary declaration, and I would close out my morning routine with that.

During this second time around, the days seemed to be shorter. There was something good about the familiarity. I had my TV listening schedule down pat; I was still engaged at work, speaking with my staff and reps daily, and keeping my sales numbers on par with what they'd been before the surgeries, and I had my meditation time. Every day was a micro victory.

Our twice-a-week visits to the doctors also helped the days to pass faster. Every Monday we ventured out to Dr. Chang, and on Thursday, we saw Dr. Freilich. But those weren't our only doctor visits.

Like I said, this time I was far more paranoid. If there was any shift in my vision, I made the call to the doctor. Tina was right there with me, agreeing that we weren't taking any chances. Any little thing I noticed, she wanted to have it checked out.

"It doesn't hurt to be careful," she said, so we had two or three extra visits to the "on-call" doctors on weekends.

Each time we were sent home with the same words— everything looks fine—and that was good enough for me.

We were coming up on July Fourth, a holiday that was very special to us because Tina and I always attended a picnic in Palisades State Park that was put together by our good friend Franklin. This was something we'd done for several years now, and it was a summer event that we really looked forward to. The July Fourth picnic was huge, with upwards of a hundred people attending. Over the years we'd invited our family, friends, and people from our couples' group. Now, it had become a tradition that everyone looked forward to.

This year, though, as the holiday approached, I contemplated whether I should go. There were so many reasons why attending was a good idea. The bubble inside my eye was dissolving, I had about twenty-five percent vision. I no longer had to keep my head down, but it still felt like there was a discotheque going on in my eye. I had some sight, so physically, I felt as if I could handle it; mentally, I thought it would be good for both Tina and me to get out and do something fun.

I believed we could handle this. I'd seen Dr. Chang and Dr. Freilich twice and had been given the "everything looks good" clearance by both of them. There really wasn't any reason not to go—except I had the same apprehensions as when I went to the meeting after the first surgery. The thought of people judging me or making fun of my condition, along with the possibility of folks asking me a million questions, was frightening.

In the end, I decided I couldn't allow what other people might say or think to stop me.

When I told Tina I wanted to go to the picnic, she asked, "Are you sure?"

Once I'd gone through all the pros and cons in my head, I was absolutely sure. "I need to get out of the house, and I need to do something to normalize my situation."

"Okay," she said, and I could tell she was happy about going to the July Fourth celebration as well.

We began thinking about the best way to attend the picnic (which would be on Saturday, July 1 this year) without putting too much pressure on Tina or myself. There was no way we could transport all of our picnic gear with just us two, so I called one of my best friends/brothers, John Moyler. I'd known John for more than forty years.

When I called John and told him I needed his help throughout that day, I let him know that the day would begin early because he'd have to help us transport all the food and picnic gear from home.

"Come on, man! What do you need my help for?"

I chuckled. John had been this way since we were kids. He always gave me a hard time, but in the end, I could always count on him. All I had to do was sit back and let him complain for a few minutes, all the while knowing that when he finished, he would show up.

So, I listened to him until he got to the part where he asked me, "What time do you need me to be there? You know I've got you. Whatever you need."

When I hung up from John, I knew I'd made the right decision to go.

As he promised, John was at our house early, around eight-thirty on the Saturday of the picnic. From the moment he arrived, he became my eyes and muscle for the entire day. He did everything, from loading the grill, tables, tents, food, and drinks into both of our trucks. Then, he followed Tina and me to Palisades Interstate Park. The park was a beautiful two-thousand-five-hundred-acre stretch of scenic land, sitting in the shadows of the George Washington Bridge. I loved coming to this place.

At the park, John went to work unloading both trucks and then setting it all up. After that, he led me around, guiding me, letting me know where we were, who was saying hello, and what was going on. Because of John, I didn't miss a thing.

The day got even better when all my childhood friends showed up. Dave, Al, Torin, and Jason were guys I'd known for over forty years as well, so getting together with them was guaranteed to be a good time. We laughed and joked and hung out like we did back in the day.

For the entire day I was surrounded by love, the same feeling I had when I'd gone to the meeting for Fernando after my first surgery. The reservations I'd had about people staring and asking lots of questions were gone. Sure, there were a few who wondered what was going on with me—maybe three or four asked questions. It was nothing I couldn't handle, and it was overshadowed by all the love I felt. There was not a bit of pity; I was treated the same as everyone else there, and that meant so much to me.

One of the best things about the day for me—was Tina. For once, I wasn't my wife's responsibility. I was in good hands with John and the guys, so it was a major break for her; she was able to have fun with her girlfriends. It was a day of relaxation where she didn't have to be concerned about anything.

This was another micro victory for me.

It was well after dark when John made sure we were home safely, and then he headed out. He had been by my side the entire day, there till the very end. My ride or die, just like I knew he would be.

Once John left, Tina and I sat together and reflected on the long day. It had been great for both of us; a major accomplishment, another milestone, another empowering experience.

I needed that love; I needed that normalcy, and I was so grateful I'd pushed past the fear and anxiety so I could have all of that. What a day this had been.

CHAPTER 19

Tina and I were still on a high from the picnic. We needed that celebration to get us back into a flow of some type of normal existence.

I still couldn't see well. Even though I was able to hold my head up, with the way the bubble was positioned, I was only able to see through the bottom of it. For the entire time at the picnic, all I could see for the most part were people's feet.

However, I didn't focus on what I hadn't been able to do. I kept my attention on what I'd done and the good feeling I had all day.

The next day was filled with a lot of prayer and a lot of mediation. I thanked God for the blessings I had and looked forward to seeing Dr. Chang later in the week.

The trip into the city on Thursday morning had become a routine for me and Tina. I was far more independent as I moved than I'd been with the first surgery because I'd memorized where to turn, where to lower my head, how to slip into the car.

On the ride to Dr. Chang's office, I reflected on how much had changed from the last time. Back then I'd been filled with anxiety and paranoia, but I was on my way back to being normal and that made me feel so optimistic.

Once we arrived in the city, I was feeling so good as we waited for Dr. Chang. As I sat and reflected, it was clear how important interaction with other people had been on this journey. My brother and Smitty had been crucial to my getting through this, and even the interaction I had with my job had been a positive distraction for me.

But the most important interaction had come this past Saturday, and days later, I was still riding high.

When we were called back to see Dr. Chang, Tina sat on the side, quiet as always, although I knew she was hopeful like me. I was prepped by the assistant, and then Dr. Chang came in being his usual kind, but very professional, self.

After all the greetings, he began the examination. He shined that coal miner's light into my eye and it was uncomfortable, but not as intense as it had been over the years.

"Okay, look up," Dr. Chang said. "Now to the left...to the right...look down."

He clicked off the light and while I'd expected a smile from him, all I heard was a small sigh.

"Steven, I don't like what I'm seeing."

There aren't words to describe how I felt at that moment. All the anxiety I'd worked so hard to get rid of rushed back like a tidal wave. I didn't even ask Dr. Chang any questions; it was shock that kept me silent.

Dr. Chang said, "We're going to have to go back in." For the first time since we'd been working together, I heard just a bit of emotion from the doctor. I wasn't able to look up into his face, but I heard his frustration and I heard his anger. It even felt as if I could hear his thoughts; it was as if he was saying, "Come on, now; we're going to have to do this again?"

He continued, "I want to get this done as soon as possible."

"How soon?" That was the only question I had within me.

"Let's get you on the schedule right away."

He stepped out of the office for a moment, and I counted back to when I'd had the second surgery. Today was July 6 and I'd just had surgery on Father's Day, barely three weeks before.

The silence felt so heavy between Tina and me, and I wanted to say something to my wife, but I didn't have anything in me. This was tough. There were too many emotions inside of me to have a conversation right now. I imagined that Tina felt the same.

By the time Dr. Chang returned, he was back to his normal self, speaking with little emotion. He told us that the surgery was scheduled for tomorrow, Friday afternoon.

"I'm so sorry, Steve," he said, his frustration gone. Now, his concern was all about me. "I wish we didn't have to do this, but I just don't like the way it looks."

"I understand," I said, thinking it was better for me to be safe and take care of any issues now. But a third time?

"This time we're going to use the silicone oil." Dr. Chang began explaining what that meant. I remembered Dr. Wald telling me in great detail about the silicone oil, but the message I took from Dr. Chang's explanation was that the gas bubble in my eye now wasn't supporting the retina enough to heal. "I know this isn't good news, but there is some consolation to this. With the silicone oil, you won't have to keep your head down as long."

Yes, that was good news. In the middle of what felt like an emotional disaster, at least I had that. "How long will I have to keep my head down?"

"Well, I won't know until after the surgery, but probably only about a week or so. With this oil, you'll be able to see a lot better and a lot faster, even with your head down. The only thing is that we will have to do a second surgery to take the oil out, which is why silicone is never my first choice."

I remembered Dr. Wald telling me that part also.

"But this will be better. In the meantime, Dr. Freilich and I will continue to keep a very close eye on you."

His next words were familiar again: he'd have his people call me and prep me for the surgery.

We said our goodbyes and Tina and I prepared to make the familiar return to the garage. At first, when we got inside the car, we said nothing. I fought hard to keep my emotions in check. I couldn't break down. I couldn't lose it in any way because of Tina. I was concerned about her and she'd totally feed off my energy.

It was a battle to remain calm, though, because there were a plethora of feelings circling inside of me: shock, anguish, even 'Fuck, not this again.' I wasn't even sure what got to me the most: having the surgery...once again, or the aftermath of the whole head down recovery process...once again.

Finally, after we'd been in the car for a while, Tina said, "I'm so sorry."

Through all the thoughts circling in my head, I was able to conjure up a bit of acceptance. I said, "It is what it is. Let's just do this. Let's just get it done." I was trying to stay outside of my feelings, even though the emotions definitely remained.

Tina said, "Okay, you're right. Let's just get it done."
And then the car returned to silence.

At home, it was all familiar again, except it wasn't. I was facing a third surgery and so what I was feeling was completely new. There were so many calls that I had to make. The first one was to Dr. Freilich, but I didn't want to call him, so I texted: My retina is leaking again and I have to have another surgery tomorrow.

There was a sense of shock and sorrow in his reply. I was sure he couldn't believe it, especially since my retina looked fine the last time he examined me.

Then I had to call Alex...again. When I called Alex, I could tell he was surprised, too. The energy on the call wasn't hostile, but I felt as if there was an awkward detachment in our conversation. I was tired of saying the same thing, and I guessed Alex was tired of hearing it.

When I hung up, I heard Tina in the living room. She had probably already emailed her office. Now she was on the phone with her support system: first, our daughter, Rachel, and her cousin, Stephanie.

I turned to my support system as well. First on my list was my brother.

"I'm just tired," I said before I explained how I was faced with a third surgery. "I'm just tired," I repeated when I got to the end. "Really tired."

There wasn't much more to that conversation because when I finished venting, there was silence from the other end of the telephone. I knew what was happening; my brother was in shock. He didn't know what to say to me.

I think he sensed that I didn't need much advice. What I needed the most was a listening ear, and he gave me that. He allowed me to have my moment, have my feelings, have the space to speak out all of my frustrations.

That was what I needed the most in this situation. Because of how I am, I just needed to talk it out so that I could work it out. I needed to talk in order to flush out what I was thinking and feeling, and I didn't want to do that with Tina. She was down in the trenches with me and there was already enough on her. She didn't need the burden of carrying my emotions, so my brother gave me that space.

I did the same thing with Smitty when I called him. I just talked and got all of my feelings, all of my emotions, out. Smitty's calm and serene presence came through the phone. He talked to me a little more than my brother did, helping again me to see God's plan and the fact that no matter what I faced, there was no way I was going to give up. With his help, I talked myself into my own solution, into my own serenity.

By the time I hung up, I was in a much better place, but it hadn't been easy. Not after coming off of such an emotional high from the weekend. Not after feeling like I was back on the road to being normal again. After that good time, Dr. Chang's words had hit me like a brick upside my head.

All I could do now was pick myself up and get to the other side.

That night my prayer routine was a little different. I usually sat in a chair in the living room facing east. But that night, I got down on my knees and when I opened my mouth to speak with God, I didn't try to hide the bit of anger that was inside of me. What would have been the point? He knew I was angry and so I let Him hear it.

I began my prayer with, "God, I need this to be over and I'm calling on You like I've never called on You before. Because enough is enough." I had never prayed to God that way. I never had that kind of anger inside of me when I talked to Him, or maybe what I felt wasn't anger. Maybe it was just passion because there was one thing I knew...while I was emotionally stretched, my faith remained, it never wavered.

But faith didn't suppress my feelings, and faith didn't stop my exhaustion. I was tired for me and for Tina, who wasn't suffering through this physically, but she experienced the same mental anguish.

So, I took all of this to God—how I was feeling, how Tina was feeling, and how neither one of us would be able to take too much more of this.

After I got it all out, I slid into bed. It was interesting, I felt much better after having that little talk with my Higher Power.

I plugged my ears with my earbuds and while Tina slept, I lay there listening to Conversations with God. I related to this story by Neale Donald Walsch because it was about a man who'd been down on his luck. He'd lost almost everything, and he began writing letters to God. In that process, he had a spiritual experience where God began to answer him and he began writing down the conversations. Once God started speaking, he asked God questions far beyond his personal circumstances; he asked God about life.

I related to his feelings surrounding his hardships and his connection to God. Listening to this book filled me with an even greater sense of peace. I was grateful for that because it was important to me that, even in the midst of all of this, in the middle of what I was feeling, in the center of my anger, I never wanted anything to get in the way of my relationship with God. I never wanted to stop what I called my spiritual maintenance. No matter what happened, I was going to continue to feed myself positivity. I knew I would have moments, and I would allow myself to have them. But then, I'd move on. I was going to continue affirming, meditating, and praying.

As I listened to the book, I scrolled through my affirmations in my mind:

My vision is 20/20.

My retina is healed, completely healed.

My retina is healthy.

I believed what I was saying because I was speaking from faith. Those were my affirmations and to this day, I believe I spoke my healing into existence.

I pushed aside all negativity: I never, again, saw myself walking with a cane. I saw myself driving. I saw myself playing with my granddaughter. I saw myself speaking publicly and sharing in meetings. I saw myself saying to people, "It's really good to see you," and meaning it on such a deeper level than most would understand.

I was ready. I was ready to face the third surgery.

CHAPTER 20

The next morning was surreal. I got up, got dressed, and prepared. Again, this was all so familiar…except this was my third surgery and that put me into an even more somber space.

Tina and I were subdued as we moved. We walked as if we carried heavy burdens and I could almost hear that good old-fashioned Negro spiritual music playing as if it were the soundtrack to my life at this moment. I didn't know the words to any of the songs, but I could hear it; I could hear the people singing about how no matter what, they would make it through, 'cause trouble didn't last always.

Once I was dressed, I left Tina alone in the bedroom and went into the living room. I faced the windows, wanting to "see" the sunrise. As I sat feeling the warmth of the sun as it began to peek above the horizon, I talked to God some more. My words weren't filled with the passion of the night before, but still, I talked to him, affirming, thanking, proclaiming, declaring…just being positive that I was about to have a successful surgery.

"Thank you, God, for guiding the hand of Dr. Chang, and thank you, God, that this will be the last one."

When Tina told me she was ready, I put my earbuds in, wanting to keep that meditation music in my head as we made the trip into the city. This time the drive seemed so long. I was grateful when Tina occasionally broke the silence.

"Are you okay?"

"Yeah, I'm good," I said, which is what I would have said even if I wasn't. I wanted to give Tina what she needed at this moment. I wanted to make sure that she didn't fall apart emotionally and by focusing on her, I kept myself together.

Once we arrived at the hospital, it was almost as if we were a celebrity couple. The familiar faces greeted us as if we were good friends. It started in the garage with the attendant, Papi, who always took care of us, even as he greeted us in his broken English.

Inside, it was the same with the security guards and all the medical staff. I'd been coming here for such a long time now that we had developed a relationship with all of them. I always did my best to compliment everyone on their professionalism. It was easy to do that because the people on this team really did a good job and did their best to take care of me. I engaged with them, having short conversations and keeping them laughing with my one-liners.

Everyone spoke to us the way they always did. "Hello, Mr. King, Mrs. King."

I knew most assumed we were there for just another appointment, but when they discovered I was back for another surgery, I felt the mood change. There was shock; no one knew what to say. I imagined some of them had the same emotions

127

as Dr. Chang—what is going on? But one thing I knew for sure—they all wished me the best.

The West Indian woman who had performed my patient intake before had me and Tina sit in front of her again as we filled out the paperwork. She tagged me with the wristband before she took me and Tina into the room.

When we were left alone, Tina got right on her phone. She wasn't speaking to anyone, so I assumed that she was texting our daughter, Rachel, Cousin Stephanie, and everyone else, letting them all know we had arrived at the hospital. This was the way she kept herself focused—she provided updates so she wouldn't have to think too much about what was to come.

As Tina texted, I kept my earbuds in, still meditating. Listening to soothing sounds that I imagined played inside spas, too, helped to keep me serene.

I remained quiet, saying my affirmations. Every couple of minutes or so, Tina would say something like, "Nachele says hi," letting me know our cousin was reaching out to check on me.

Tina sounded calm, but as hard as I had been trying with my meditating, anxiety began to creep in. I think it was all the waiting. I was just ready to get up to the operating room so that this could be done.

Finally, a nurse came in with my change of clothes: the gown, the socks, the plastic cap, and then, I had to wash my face. I changed into my surgical clothes and gave my watch and wallet to Tina. I put my earbuds back in and now I was listening to Joel Osteen.

Once the nurse came in to put in my eye drops, I began to block out all thoughts, focusing my energy on staying positive;

that was what my prayers, meditation, and affirmations were all about. I channeled all my emotions into one place—a feeling of peace.

Once the nurse finished, I was asked what felt like dozens of questions:

"When is the last time you had something to eat?"

"What did you eat?"

"So, you had nothing this morning?"

There were times when I wanted to say, "Why are you asking me all of these questions?" They knew I was aware of the routine; they knew I followed the instructions and wouldn't break any of the rules. With this being my third time, I felt like I could be the one asking the questions. However, even though I just wanted to get into the operation room, I knew the nurses were just doing their jobs—and doing their jobs well. I was more than appreciative because mistakes could happen.

It was as if everything was timed because right after that, the anesthesiologist came in and introduced himself. "I'll be in the room when they bring you up," he said before he left us alone.

His appearance made me feel the weight of this again. A few minutes later, another West Indian woman came in with a wheelchair.

"Okay, it's time to take you up," she sang in that musical Caribbean lilt.

I kissed Tina and she told me she would see me in a few minutes. This time, for some reason, she would be able to come into the operating room. As the nurse rolled me out of the room and then down the hall, she seemed to know everyone that we passed. She had at least a dozen little side conversations by the time we entered the elevator.

Within minutes, though, I was once again in the operating room. For a moment, I paused and took in all that was familiar—the cooler temperatures in the room, the compressions sound wheezing from the machines to the chatter that was much softer on this floor.

After I'd been helped onto the table, the anesthesiologist said, "Okay, Mr. King, you're going to feel a little pinch." He inserted the IV for the sedative. I would be awake for this surgery, but this would keep me mellow and it slowed down any involuntary movements such as sneezes or coughs that could negatively affect the surgery.

Once again the nurses put on my compression socks and then covered me with a warm blanket that felt as if it had just been lifted from the oven. At the same time, I felt the tingling of the medicine traveling through my vein as a nurse hooked me up to the EKG machine.

"Are you okay, Mr. King?"

"I'm fine."

"Are you cold?"

"No, I'm fine with this blanket."

"Do you need a pillow?"

"No, I'm fine."

If I hadn't been comfortable, the surgical team would have found a way to make it happen for me.

"Okay, well, Dr. Chang is prepping, he will be right with you."

Right then, Tina came in and kissed me on my forehead. "Are you okay, honey?"

"Yeah, I'm good," I said, wondering if they'd have to clean my forehead again. I said, "I love you, babe. I'll see you in a little while." I paused. "You get it? I'll see you in a little while?"

All Tina did was shake her head, but here's the thing— that line made her smile and that's all I wanted. I could tell that her seeing me on the surgical table made her a little emotional, and for a moment, I wanted to give her that reprieve.

Tina walked out of the room and Dr. Chang came in. It was time to get this third surgery started.

CHAPTER 21

"Steve, hopefully, this is the last time we'll have to do this," Dr. Chang said.

"I hope so."

"Well, we're going to try something different this time. We're not going to use the gas bubble. We're going to use the silicone oil."

Dr. Chang had told me this already, but just like everyone else, he was a professional and explained everything thoroughly, at least twice.

"Hopefully, the silicone will support your retina a lot better than the gas bubble."

He spoke with a bit of enthusiasm as if he was rooting for me.

The anesthesiologist said, "We're going to begin so you'll start to feel relaxed."

Before Dr. Chang began, he introduced me to the resident who would be helping him this time. As Dr. Chang began, he explained to his resident my situation. He went through everything, from the fact that I'd been severely nearsighted as a child, to the macular hole and how he'd fixed it, but how there had been leakage afterward.

He mentioned that I had a 37-millimeter eye, which is something I'd known, but the way Dr. Chang said it, it sounded kind of like I had the unicorn of eyes, I guessed.

Once he was done, he said, "Okay, Steve, we're going to start. And hopefully, this is the last time."

Hopefully, I thought.

As he began, I felt the way I had the first time—weird. It was because I was awake and could see Dr. Chang, at least the outline of his body. But I couldn't feel a thing, which was good since Dr. Chang was making an incision in my eye. Like before, I could see the shadow of instruments.

I tried to stop thinking about what was happening, not wanting to focus on all the things that could freak me out: the fact that this was the third time and suppose this didn't work? I did what I'd trained myself to do through meditation and prayer—I became numb in the moment and in that peace, I began to think about my mother. I knew that she was watching over me; I knew she wasn't going to allow anything bad to happen to me.

At least an hour had passed when Dr. Chang said, "Okay, we're just about done here. We're just going to put the silicone oil in and hopefully, this should do it."

I wanted to say, 'Damn, Doc, hopefully?' But inside, I chuckled. Dr. Chang would always put a disclaimer on everything. His words were never definite, never filled with promises he wasn't sure he could keep.

Dr. Chang was standing close to me when he finally told me he was done. What was amazing was that I could see him!

I breathed with relief as they patched up my eye and within twenty minutes, I was wheeled back to the room where I was assisted into the bed.

Through my grogginess that remained because of the anesthesia, I heard, "Honey, are you okay?"

Like always, that was the sweetest sound.

A few minutes later another nurse came into the room with apple juice and Graham crackers. About a half-hour after that, Dr. Chang entered.

"How are you doing, Steve?"

"I feel fine."

"Well, everything went well, and I hope this is the last time we have to do this."

Again, there was that disclaimer. I understood why he spoke this way, but just once, this one time, I hoped for something that he couldn't give to me—certainty.

"Now with the silicone oil, you'll keep your head down for a couple of days, but it will be nowhere near as long as with the gas bubble."

I nodded. No matter how many times he told me that, I felt great each time I heard it.

"So, I'll see you tomorrow," Dr. Chang said.

Before I let Dr. Chang walk out of the room, I asked him like I'd done the last two times: "How should I lie my head when I sleep?"

Even though I'd been through this two other times, I wanted clarity. Dr. Chang showed me how to sleep on my right side and then said that he'd see us the next day. About forty-five minutes later, a nurse came in with the drops and all the instructions, once again.

As I sat up to get dressed, my eye began to throb. It was a bit shocking because I'd never had pain before. But I ignored it, thinking it was just a headache.

This time, when we were inside the car, I was quiet because I just didn't want to talk. All I told Tina was, "I just want to get home, get something to eat, and lie down."

My head was still throbbing when we got to the apartment. I rested while Tina ordered food for us. When our order arrived, I enjoyed that turkey sandwich before I swallowed a couple of ibuprofens and went fast asleep.

When I finally woke up, I didn't know the time. We'd gotten home so late I didn't know if I'd only slept for an hour or longer. My head was still throbbing and I wondered why I had this headache.

I called out to Tina; I needed help to go to the bathroom. Once I was inside there, I removed the patch from my eye. My vision wasn't totally clear, but it was much better than the gas bubble and that grape Kool-Aid. Now, it felt like I was peering through water that was wavy, but definitely clear.

This was the blessing part of the third surgery. Being able to see through something that looked like clear water would allow me to maneuver and navigate through the house much faster because, even when my head was down, I could see, I could definitely see. Standing in front of the mirror, I felt like I had my first victory for this go-round.

CHAPTER 22

The next morning the headache was gone. That was good, but what was better was that I could see! Having the oil in my eye was so different; even getting dressed felt like a new experience.

Because of being able to see, I felt a bit more upbeat as I dressed for my eight o'clock post-operation appointment with Dr. Chang. That subtle change gave me a lot of hope.

The appointment wasn't at the office on 53rd Street. Since this was a Saturday, we met Dr. Chang at the hospital. As Tina drove, I did my usual meditation and I was so grateful to be able to see. However, gratitude wasn't the only thing I was feeling. Like with my past surgeries, I wondered if this would work. I wondered if this would be the last time.

At the hospital we had to wait in the lobby for Dr. Chang—he was making a special trip in for this appointment. As we waited, I tried to push away thoughts of Dr. Chang examining me and seeing something wrong—again. This had to be the final time because I didn't know how much more of this I could take—physically, mentally, and emotionally.

I felt a little bit better once Dr. Chang arrived. By the time he took us to his office and sat me in the examination chair, I was calm, but admittedly, I was also a little tense.

Dr. Chang sat on his stool and rolled over to me. "Steve, I really hope this is the last time we have to do this because I can only imagine what you're going through."

His voice was tinged with just a bit of emotion. This was only the second time I'd heard that from the strait-laced doctor.

I said, "I hope so, too."

He turned on the bright light and it felt like he was shining it on that one question that remained with me: Would Dr. Chang discover something that would set me back again?

After a couple of silent seconds, he said, "There's a little blood in the corner of your eye."

"What do you mean?" I asked, wondering if this was the problem I feared.

Then, in a tone that didn't sound like he was concerned at all, he said, "It's normal. It's just in the inner part of your eye and your eye is a little puffy, but that will go down. It's just inflammation."

He spoke matter-of-factly and I took my cue from him. He went through all the instructions, telling me to look up, down, to the left, to the right.

When he finished, I held my breath until he said, "Okay, your eye looks good."

I exhaled.

Dr. Chang said, "I think the oil will support your retina better." He added, "You'll just keep your head down for the next five days until I see you again on Thursday." He recapped the instructions he'd given me yesterday, including how I would need to wear the clear shell any time I walked around my apartment. "And wear it when you're sleeping," he said. "You can take the bandage off when you get home, but keep the shell on."

"Definitely," I said.

"I want you to start seeing Dr. Freilich again. I'll call and update him on your condition. If you can follow up and call him on Monday, I'd like you to see him on Tuesday."

As Tina and I prepared to leave, Dr. Chang said, "I'm really sorry you had to go through all of this, but hopefully this time we got it right."

Those were his parting words, once again giving me a glimpse into his human side. I was grateful because he cared, but most of all, I was grateful for all he'd done for me.

As she drove us home, Tina kept me focused on the good news: the surgery had gone well, I could see better, and this pain in my neck would be over in five days, not two weeks.

"And just think," Tina said, "when you go to sleep tonight and wake up tomorrow, it will only be four more days."

I laughed. She was always focused on the positive and she was right. I was in a good place and our mood on the ride home showed that.

It was still pretty early when we arrived back at the apartment, so I rested for the remainder of the morning before I got up to feast on my favorite meal, that turkey sandwich with fries.

Afterward, I called Smitty and my brother, wanting to share the good news of my doctor's appointment. Over these months, they'd had to hear my despair; today, I wanted to share my hope.

As I talked to my support system, of course, Tina was on her phone calls with the people who supported her. I imagined that she wanted to share the good news, too. It had been a good morning, a good afternoon. Just an overall good day.

Everything was wonderful, until I woke up Sunday morning. It wasn't apparent at first. When I got up about six, or six-thirty, I had planned to just go through my regular routine. I was able to get up easily enough and maneuver around.

I went into the living room to do my spiritual routine and bask in the warmth of the early morning sun and the silence. But as I sat there, I noticed something in my eye—the oil seemed different from the day before, it kept shifting. At first, I tried to ignore it, but there was definitely something going on. I tried to push down my concern, but after an hour or so, I was so paranoid that I couldn't take it anymore.

Maybe it was just because I was able to see now; maybe the oil was a blessing and a curse when compared to the gas bubble where I couldn't see anything in the beginning. Because with being able to see, I was looking for any and everything that even remotely reminded me of that Saturday before Father's Day, the day I unfondly referred to as the Father's Day Massacre.

So much was going on in my eye. There were shifts and changes, those floaters again, like flashing lights in a '70s disco. I'd experienced all of this before, but this time it seemed to be excessive. If I'd taken the time to really think about it, the changes were probably good, probably just part of the healing process and the only reason I was seeing these changes was that I could see.

All of that was reasonable, but it was hard for me to be sensible at this moment. My paranoia told me these changes weren't good, and that I was once again about to experience the Father's Day Massacre.

There was no way I could talk myself down because there was no way to ignore what was right in front of my eyes, literally. So instead of focusing on the shift in my eye, I tried to shift my thinking. That didn't help either and my anxiety continued to rise until it reached a crescendo and I crashed. The only thing I could do was take this all to God.

I went to Him the same way I did the night before this third surgery. I spoke to God with the same passion, but I laid it all out. I'd been through so much; not just this time, but since I was a child. This had been going on for too many years. I wasn't angry at God, but when I cried out to Him with tears in my eyes, all I could say was, "Enough is enough." How much was one person supposed to take?

After I prayed, I reached for the phone. I had to call the doctor. Like all the times before, I called the emergency number, and when the operator came on, I gave her my name, number, and all the information I'd given the half dozen other times I called: I was a patient of Dr. Chang's, I'd just had surgery for the third time, something was wrong.

"I don't like what I'm seeing," I told her.

I heard the keys on the computer clicking as she entered all of my information.

"Okay," she said, "just stay calm."

I guessed she could hear my mental temperature was rising. After she finished transcribing all I'd told her, she said, "Someone will call you back shortly."

Right as I hung up, Tina came into the living room. "What's going on?"

Turning to her, I really hated to say anything. This was too much, too much for me, and too much for her. I saw the concern in her eyes, I heard that same concern in her tone, and…I lost it. I had kind of a breakdown.

I explained to Tina what was going on, and for the first time ever, I couldn't control my emotions. As I spoke, I paced, trying to compose myself, but I couldn't. I'd worked hard not to get emotional in front of Tina, but this time, I didn't have that within me.

Tina tried to console me as best she could. She'd never seen me like this so I was sure she had no idea what to say.

It felt like an eternity passed as I tried to pull myself back from this emotional edge. When the telephone finally rang about ten minutes later, I stopped moving.

After the doctor introduced herself, I explained what was going on and what I was seeing.

"Well," she began after I paused, "you know there are going to be shifts. With the oil, there will be floaters in your eyes. How is your vision?"

"It's pretty much the same," I said, and then for a moment, I wondered: Had I just overreacted?

The doctor said, "That's a strong indicator that what you're seeing may not be anything serious. With the oil, things are magnified, so this really sounds pretty normal for someone who just had surgery with the silicone oil."

Her words calmed me, gave me the reassurance I needed to come up from my breakdown. She was talking me into believing that everything was okay.

The doctor continued, "I think it's fine. What I want you to do is just monitor it and if you see any drastic changes, then call me back."

I believed the doctor, but only to a point. What I really wanted was for this doctor to tell me to get to a hospital, just so I could be sure. However, I didn't want to drag my wife out of the house at eight o'clock on a Sunday morning. Especially not after a doctor had just told me I was fine.

After hanging up I was no longer on the ledge, but there were still all these different voices in my head and I wasn't sure which one I should listen to—was I going to be fine or not?

I tried to settle my thoughts. The doctor's explanation made sense, and although she was like every other doctor and couldn't tell me that I was definitely going to be all right, she'd given me a logical reason for what I was seeing.

I told Tina what the doctor said, but at first, she didn't respond. I knew it was because she just wasn't sure what to do, how to help. She'd never seen me panic before and now, I was upset that I'd done that to her. I was filled with new emotions: shame and guilt for having done this to my wife.

Once we ate and I rested for a while, I was back to normal—or what could be considered normal in this situation. It was the most anxiety I'd had throughout this entire experience. I'd never had an emotional moment like that before...and I was blessed not to have another one again.

CHAPTER 23

Following Dr. Chang's instructions, on Monday morning I called to schedule an appointment with Dr. Freilich for Tuesday. Now I was even more grateful for this plan because after what happened the day before, there was no way I'd be able to wait until Thursday when I would see Dr. Chang.

Going to Dr. Freilich's office was a much different and much easier trip than going to Dr. Chang's. Twenty minutes after leaving our apartment, we were in his suburban office. There, I was greeted with the same compassion I always felt from the staff. Today I could feel their sympathy, as if they knew I'd already been through so much.

Their kindness, though, never eased my waiting room anxiety. There were knots in my stomach as I wondered what would happen if I'd been right over the weekend. Suppose there was something really wrong with my eye and the doctor had missed it?

By the time Dr. Freilich greeted me and Tina in the examination room, my thoughts had taken me right back to the edge. He said, "You sure have been through a lot, Steve."

He then turned his attention to Tina and asked how she was doing.

I was so grateful that he acknowledged my wife and the role she'd played in this journey. He knew she was going through all of this with me.

After that, Dr. Freilich only had encouraging words, like always. "I've said this before and I'll say it again. You're in the best hands possible. If anyone can pull you through this, it's Dr. Chang."

That was something I knew, but a much-needed reminder. Dr. Freilich had become more than my eye doctor. There were times when I felt as if he stepped into the role of my therapist. From the moment I walked into his office that first time, he was rooting for me, and willing to play his part and do whatever he had to do to help in whatever way he could.

"Okay, now let me take a look at that eye."

First, Dr. Freilich had me to read the vision chart. I could see the letters even though they were wavy.

With that bright light and magnifying glass, he checked my retina, asking me to look up, down, to the left, then the right. The light was more intense now, but I understood that. The gas bubble blocked some of the brightness, but the oil, with its transparency, didn't give me much protection.

"Okay, everything looks good. Let's go take a picture of your eye."

For something that normally took four to five minutes, this time Dr. Freilich couldn't get a clear image of my eye. Before I could ask what was wrong, Dr. Freilich explained.

"It's because of the oil; I can't get a good picture of the retina. The oil is distorting the photograph. When you see Dr.

Chang on Thursday, you'll have to tell him I couldn't get the image, but everything else looked fine."

We made an appointment for the following Tuesday and when I walked out of his office, I felt comforted. Except for not being able to get the image, this was all good news. Tina thought so, too.

"Everything looks good," she said, repeating Dr. Freilich's words once we were in the car. "And now just a few more days before you'll be able to keep your head up."

This was Tina's nature—to encourage me and keep me motivated. I was sure she was encouraging herself as well. Now, all we had to do was wait two days, and then it would be time to see Dr. Chang.

With the silicone oil in my eye, my life was easier, and that included calling into work.

The women on my team were running the show in the office, but I was still dealing with my reps, closing deals, and helping them through any challenges. I wasn't sleeping during the day as much as I had with the first two surgeries, so in-between sales calls and other work check-ins, I'd check out my favorites on TV: News, Sports Center, and The Wendy Williams Show.

In the evening I'd check in with my brother and Smitty, and on this night, I was glad to share the good news from Dr. Freilich. I just hoped that the rest of my conversations with them would be the same.

And then, Thursday came…it was time for Dr. Chang.

CHAPTER 24

Of course, I knew Dr. Chang was the best in the world, but that didn't stop me from feeling anxious on that Thursday morning. He had helped me through so much, but at the same time, all the bad news I'd ever received about my eye during this journey came through him.

So on Thursday morning, I even woke up apprehensive. I felt as if there was so much on the line. Not only because of what I'd been through on Sunday, but because this was a big day. If all went well, I'd be able to lift my head, hopefully never to put it down again.

Usually, by the time I walked into Dr. Chang's office, I had my paranoia under control. Not today. The entire time I sat with the assistant who did all the preliminaries, I felt as if I was just one large ball of nerves.

Like with Dr. Freilich, taking the image of my eye seemed to be a bit more challenging than before. But eventually, they were able to get what they needed.

Now, it was more waiting and waiting and waiting for Dr. Chang. I never had to wait very long, but today my nervousness made the five minutes feel like five days.

I needed to do something, so I closed my eyes and did what I'd learned years before with Tony Robbins when I attended one of his conferences in Colorado Springs. One of his techniques was visualization—to visualize the outcome you wanted. I'd learned how to do that with an exercise where he had the attendees walking across hot coals.

Before we did that exercise, we visualized getting to the other side, taking our focus from the heat of the coals and turning our attention to the outcome we wanted—getting to the other side and visualizing the celebration at the end.

So, that's what I did as I sat there; I used that technique, visualizing the words I wanted to hear from Dr. Chang. Everything looks good. I visualized the relief I would feel afterward.

I repeated those words, seeing and hearing Dr. Chang in my mind. As I did that, all those negative feelings inside of me began to subside. By the time I sat in front of Dr. Chang, I had control of my emotions.

After greeting me and Tina, Dr. Chang asked, "So, how did your appointment go on Tuesday?"

"It was good," I said, although I didn't want to chat. I always loved talking to Dr. Chang, but today, all I wanted was for him to study my eye and tell me what he thought.

"I spoke to Dr. Freilich, and he told me that everything was okay."

"Yeah, he said everything was fine; he just had a little trouble getting a good image of my eye."

"Really?" Dr. Chang said with a bit of surprise in his voice. Then the doctor did something that I'd seldom seen him do—he chuckled. That made me chuckle, too. There were so few times when I saw the personality of Dr. Chang. Here he was, not only chuckling, but he was doing it in an innocent kind of way.

After his little chuckle, Dr. Chang got down to business. He studied the image of my eye. "Everything looks good."

There it was, the words I'd visualized. The words I wanted and needed to hear.

He asked, "So it's been going well?"

I shared the scare I'd experienced on Sunday, complete with how I'd panicked; he listened and was understanding.

"I get it," he said when I finished. "There's a lot going on in your eye, so you're going to see shifts. The oil is adjusting and as it settles, the light hits it, causing different types of refractions and reflections. Just be prepared for a lot of that, but I can tell you, so far so good."

The next question was just as important as everything else to me. "So, you said I could lift up my head today?"

He thought for a moment. "How many days has it been?"

"Five."

"Well, let's do two more days. After Saturday you can lift your head."

Having to wait until Sunday was a little disappointing, but I guessed Dr. Chang was going to err on the safer side. I could accept that.

Then I asked, "What about the oil? You said before that I'd have to have another surgery to take that out."

"Yes, but we'll play that by ear. It'll be at least a couple of months. You don't have to worry, though. With the oil, you'll be able to see, you'll be able to function. That's one reason why I want to fit you for a new prescription."

I nodded. The prescription was to help adjust my vision with the refraction of the oil.

Then Dr. Chang added, "So maybe we can even think about going back to work soon."

Wow! It was July 13 and I'd been home for over two months. This was the best news yet.

"I'll let you know about work soon," Dr. Chang added. He continued with the rest of his instructions—how I had to continue with the eye drops, and how I should check in with Dr. Freilich on Tuesdays and then back with him every Thursday.

By the time I left the office, I felt encouraged. Two appointments in two days and two doctors told me everything was fine.

I went home feeling like just maybe I was on my way. This time when I got home, all I thought about was healing and I didn't worry about having another setback. The Father's Day Massacre and its aftermath were behind me. My eye and I were moving on.

The first major breakthrough started on Saturday night when Tina said in her sing-song voice, "Tomorrow when you wake up, you'll be able to lift your head."

The next morning, that's what I did. I lifted my head and I could see. I felt as if I'd been set free. I had a good time that day, doing things just because I could: opening the cabinets, going into the refrigerator, leaning back on the sofa, and watching television. It was a huge weight off my neck.

Dr. Chang was right about one thing, a lot was going on in my eye—those flashing lights and floaters. But now, I understood the reason and the shifts and changes didn't send me into a panic.

For the next few weeks, I continued my appointments with Dr. Freilich and Dr. Chang, and every week I was told that I was healing well. I felt that, too, because my vision was the best it had been throughout this ordeal. My vision tests were showing that I had 20/40 vision.

With this freedom of sight, life at home changed as well. Of course, Tina and I were both still working from home, but with my head up, we were able to get out of the house and do other things. We could live! Dr. Chang had saved more than my eyesight, he'd saved my quality of life.

About three weeks after having the third surgery, I received a call from Natalie, the COO of the company where I worked. While she greeted me and asked how I was doing, I could tell from her tone this was not just a general welfare-check call.

"I'm calling to get an update," she said. "What's going on, Steve? Any idea on when you're coming back?"

At first, I was a bit insulted by her question. Did she think I was home just relaxing? Did she think I wanted to be going through all of this? And for the record, while I was going through all of this, I was still working, still producing deals. Through the three surgeries, I made sure I was making it happen in the office.

Then as quickly as that thought came to me, I pushed it aside. My company didn't know what was going on...not really. Plus, making this call wasn't something Natalie would have done on her own; she was just doing what the partners asked her to do.

So, I didn't let what I was thinking show when I responded. I simply told her, "Look, Natalie, what do you want me to tell you? I had to have that third surgery and the doctor hasn't released me yet."

I must have had a little something extra in my tone because Natalie backed up and shifted the conversation.

She asked, "Well, how are you feeling?"

I told her everything was going well and I had the same goal as everyone there. I wanted to get back to work as soon as I could.

"Well, just keep us posted," she said, and then hung up.

Natalie didn't realize she and I had the same goals. I wanted this to be over because I was ready to get my whole life back, and that included going back to the office.

CHAPTER 25

Time passed and finally about a month after my third surgery, Dr. Chang released me to return to work. The thought of that filled me with anxiety...what should I expect? I wondered about all the comments and questions that would come my way. I was a man who loved attention, but at the same time, I hated it. I didn't want any attention that brought sympathy; I didn't want to deal with all the curiosity.

While I had those kinds of questions, I was prepared to do this physically. The new eyeglass prescription from Dr. Chang gave me great vision, the best I'd had in a long time. With that prescription, I'd settled into my life. I was back at meetings, although Tina still had to drive since I hadn't been released to do that yet. Nor could I work out. Everything else—life was almost like it was before my surgeries.

Now, I was ready to go back to work and face the world with my super-vision. The oil still made my sight a bit wavy, but it was subtle. It was noticeable, but not distorted, and over the weeks I'd become used to it. So my challenges returning to work weren't going to be physical at all; it was all psychological because of my image. To most in the office, I was Steven King, the guy who had kind of this superhero image, and now, I was broken down a little bit. The kryptonite had hit me, and I knew the questions would come; I would just have to face it.

Dr. Chang approved my return to work at my appointment on Thursday, August 10, and I called Alex that day to let him know I'd be returning to work the following Monday. Of course, he was glad to hear that, though his response was a bit measured.

"Okay, that's great," he said.

Those were his words, but his tone sounded a bit generic to me. I guess he'd expected my return for a while now, and maybe he wondered if it was really going to happen.

But then when Alex added, "Enjoy the weekend, Steve, and I'll see you on Monday," it became real to me.

I was glad I had Friday, Saturday, and Sunday to prepare. I wanted to focus on my excitement instead of all the things that made me anxious. This truly was an exciting time; returning to work was the final part of truly getting my life back.

By Sunday night, the excitement overwhelmed me. I went to bed feeling like a kid on Christmas Eve. I only slept sporadically.

The next morning after waking up, I got dressed for work, exactly the way I'd done my entire adult life. Tina and I planned to take the ferry into work, which was the way we commuted quite often.

Even though months had passed, it felt like just another morning on the ride to Weehawken. However, that was where

Tina and I parted. She took a different ferry that docked at the World Financial Center, closer to her job, while I was going to Midtown. She gave me a kiss, wished me luck, and then, for the first time in months, I was on my own.

It was easy enough since I could see just fine. Getting onto the ferry was no problem and it was the perfect day for this kind of ride. Summertime, calm waters…it was all very serene, very refreshing, a relaxing and perfect way to begin my first day back.

Docking on the other side of the river wasn't the end of the commute for me. I had to take a shuttle from the ferry terminal on 12th Avenue to 34th Street and 7th Avenue, which would let me off just a block from my job. Just like the ferry, that ride was comfortable and easy enough. When the shuttle stopped on 34th Street, I was ready.

Until I stepped off the bus, and the flood gates opened up.

In all of my calculations of how this day would go, I hadn't counted on arriving in Manhattan in the middle of the hustle and bustle of the morning rush hour. The moment I hit the sidewalk, a wave of people whizzed by me, running to and from their buses and trains. Every part of the city was busy at this time of the day, but in this area, it was especially frenzied because of Penn Station.

I was overwhelmed by the rush of people. It felt as if I were in the middle of a stampede and I couldn't get away. Fear filled me as people rushed by, making me feel as if I were competing on a speedway. I was so unsteady on my feet and couldn't keep up with the pace.

I was a New Yorker; how could I have forgotten this part?

My office was just a block away on 35th between Seventh and Broadway, but it was going to be a challenge to get there.

As I moved forward, people darted in and out, which made it more difficult to maneuver, especially with some of my peripheral vision gone from this last surgery. Right when I started to step off the curb, a bicycle sped by, pushing me back. People speed-walked by me, rolling suitcases, bumping into me as they passed.

In the past, the walk from the shuttle to my office took four, no longer than five minutes. But there was so much going on that my slow walk felt more like it took an hour.

By the time I arrived at my building, I was unnerved. I had made it, but I wasn't sure I'd be able to deal with that again. I hadn't even sat behind my desk yet, and already I had my first setback.

However, I had to take the small victory—I had made it to my office building and when I entered, I was greeted by the doorman.

"Hey, I haven't seen you in a while."

I braced myself. These were the moments I had prepared for—when the questions and curiosity would come. I answered, "Yeah, I've been away." I left it there because although he was a cool guy and we chatted often, we were friendly, but we weren't friends.

"Well, good to see you," he said before I got into the elevator.

That was a relief, but it wouldn't be as easy when I got to the third floor, where my colleagues would be waiting. This was the part that had brought me the most anxiety over the weekend.

I exited the elevator and moved down the long hall with much more deftness than I'd had on the street. Before I turned the corner at the end, I braced myself once again and turned. In front of me were faces I recognized, people who worked for the same company, but this was a different department.

Their glances were filled with recognition and then surprise.

"Hey." One of the guys I saw all the time was the first one to speak up. "Where have you been?"

"I had surgery," I said. "I'm just returning to work."

"Well, good to have you back," he said, though his words sounded a bit strange. He stared at me and I wondered what that was about.

The office was set up like a huge open call center, so now everyone could see me. As I passed people, some nodded, others stood to greet me. Everyone seemed so reserved, even as they said, "It's good to see you."

This subdued reaction wasn't at all what I'd been expecting. The exchanges felt awkward and I felt weird, almost as out of place as I'd felt on the street.

After I settled at my desk, I took a couple of minutes to calm myself before I went in first to see Natalie.

"Hey, Steve," she said. Her greeting was warm, but the expression on her face was strange. Almost like she was surprised about something. I couldn't imagine what, she knew I was returning today.

She invited me into her office and I told her the story of what I'd been through over these past months. She was fully engaged as she listened and was shocked as I explained surgery two and then surgery three. I could see and feel her compassion.

"So, how are you feeling now?"

"I'm good," I said, and then with a chuckle, I added, "It's really good to see you."

She chuckled, too, and I felt as if now, the ice had been broken.

Next, I met with my team, and the stiffness and awkwardness I'd felt with everyone else continued, which was really strange with this group. I'd been working with my team over the phone, so I just couldn't understand their stares filled with concern. It seemed like they were happy to see me, but everyone was guarded, almost timid.

The paranoia I had fought so hard to keep away seeped in. Something was going on. Everyone was polite, but no one seemed happy I was back as I thanked my team for holding it down. In the months that passed, my team hadn't missed a beat and I appreciated the work they'd put in to make that happen.

At one point during the meeting, Cora asked, "Are you sure you're okay?"

"Yeah," I said, frowning, wondering where the question was coming from.

She asked, "Is there something you're not telling us?"

I shook my head. Why was she asking me that question?

After that meeting I called all my reps in the field as well, letting them all know I was back in the office. Finally, I sat down with Alex. With him, it was a bit different. I didn't feel the hesitation I felt with everyone else, but I also didn't feel Natalie's compassion. Alex was more matter-of-factly, just glad I was back. Very quickly, the conversation turned to business.

"My team was able to keep up." Then I added a joke. "I was able to close sixty deals with my eyes closed."

We laughed, but Alex was pleased with that since it was higher than our normal monthly production. He told me he had a lot of respect for me, what I'd been through and had come through.

Eventually, over the weeks, the awkwardness and looks of shock and surprise went away, but it was months before I found out what was behind all of those stares of concern when I walked through the door that morning.

It was Cora who told me the reason for all the shocked reactions—it was because I'd lost so much weight. That was something I hadn't thought of, but since I hadn't been able to work out, I'd lost about fifteen pounds. It didn't seem like a big deal to me, and obviously not even to Tina, who saw me every day; to both of us, there was no drastic change. But after a three-month leave, it was a shocking change to everyone else and it made many of them believe there was more to my story; maybe I'd been very sick.

They were all happy when they realized I was fine.

On that first day of my return, I didn't get a lot of work done. I had a lot of meetings, made my rounds, checking in with everyone in the office, and did my best to get back a flow.

I had planned to stay for the entire day, but after what I experienced that morning, I didn't want to go through that in the evening rush hour. I told Natalie about my experience that morning and let her know that I would be leaving a little early to avoid that.

But my plan didn't work as well as I thought it would. Even though I left the office around three, this was New York, it was the summer, and between Penn Station and Macy's, the streets were still crowded. However, it was much easier than it had been in the morning. The ferry was almost empty and as relaxing as it had been earlier. Taking that ferry back was the perfect way to end what had been both a challenging and rewarding first day of work.

The first thing I told Tina when we met up in Weehawken was that I was exhausted. Just being out, the physicality of the travel and the stress of the morning had left me beyond tired. Actually, it was the morning commute that stuck out in my mind more than anything that happened that day. The rest of the day may have been great, but it was what had happened in the morning that made me hesitant for the next day.

However, while I had that concern, I was mindful to celebrate the victory. I'd been through a lot and I wanted to remember that. After three surgeries, I was back, and I could see. I was close to returning to my normal life completely. I needed to take the good with the bad.

My plan for the next day was that after I found a way to handle the morning commute, I wanted to completely return to my work schedule. At least all of those first awkward moments were behind me. Everyone, including me, would be more relaxed.

The next morning I still had a lot of trepidation, and the commute was still tough. However, Tuesday was better than Monday, and I hoped that each day would get better.

In the office, I was able to settle into my workflow, but even that was more taxing than I expected. The bright lights were overbearing and left me with a low-grade headache. For the first time, I realized how being away from work was different in so many ways. The office light was nothing like the soft light at home. However, I fought through it, because even though I had worked from home, there was so much to be done. I had a lot of catching up to do.

Again, I left work a little early, around four this time, and on Wednesday and Thursday, I stayed until five.

On Friday, I didn't go to work since I had an appointment with Dr. Freilich and I was a little excited about seeing him. I wanted to share all of the victories of this week and just make sure everything was still fine.

I was surprised, though, when Tina and I entered Dr. Freilich's office that morning and a bit of that old anxiety returned to me. Even though I was back at work, even though I had all of those successes, I guess it was like returning to the scene of a crime. So much trauma had occurred in doctors' offices, and I couldn't get the past out of my mind.

Those feelings dissipated once I was in front of Dr. Freilich. Excitedly, I told him about my experiences and even now, I remember the expression on his face—it was priceless. If there had been a music track to go along with that moment, it would have been the theme song from Rocky. All along, Dr. Freilich had been rooting for me, the underdog in these circumstances. But now, the energy that was coming from him—it was like he was holding his hands up in the air, cheering on my victory.

When Dr. Freilich checked my vision, he was impressed. "This is probably the best that your vision has been since I started seeing you."

He still had trouble taking an image of my eye with the oil. In fairness to Dr. Freilich, he was working in private practice in the suburbs of New Jersey. Dr. Chang was at Columbia Presbyterian. Dr. Chang definitely had more resources.

"So, you've been feeling fine? No issues?" Dr. Freilich asked me.

"None at all," I said, and then added, "except, I've been having a few headaches. But I was thinking those came from the bright lights of the office and staring at a computer all day."

As I spoke, Dr. Freilich nodded. "Yes, your eye will adjust to that. It's the strain that comes from that light."

"That's what I thought. They've just been minor headaches."

At the end of that appointment, Dr. Freilich said, "Well, Steve, I think this is it. I don't think I'll have to see you anymore. You'll be fine from here, under Dr. Chang's care."

This was definitely a bittersweet moment. Sweet because this meant I was truly getting better; I was finally on the other side. However, I hated the thought of not seeing Dr. Freilich regularly. He had been my mental stabilizer, playing such an important role for me while I was going through such a volatile period.

I guessed I was beyond that now. My retina was stable; there was no need for these double doctor visits.

Dr. Freilich said, "Steve, you're on a good roll now. I'll stay in touch with Dr. Chang."

I thanked Dr. Freilich, but there would never be a way I could thank him for all he'd done for me, especially introducing me to Dr. Chang. That was life-changing and for that, I would always be grateful.

CHAPTER 26

The next major hurdle I crossed was when I saw Dr. Chang a week later. Of course, going to see him was a routine by this time. Tina took off from work for the day to go to the appointment with me and we drove up to Columbia Presbyterian.

Since this was Thursday, there was the regular team of support people at the hospital, all the people we'd come to know, all who were our bright spots. From the security guard to the receptionist in Dr. Chang's office, their warmth always made me smile.

I walked into Dr. Chang's office and again I felt like I was returning to the scene of the crime. To overcome that as I waited, I visualized what I wanted Dr. Chang to say—how my eye was doing well. I imagined how I would cheer after he said that. I visualized the celebration.

Like with my appointment with Dr. Freilich a few days before, that anxiety went away as soon as I sat in front of Dr. Chang and he told me that all looked good.

"I'm very pleased with what's going on," he told me.

I was surprised by how relieved I felt, and now, I was looking forward to the next steps. "When do you think we'll take the oil out?"

"Let's give it a couple of more months and see how it goes."

I was okay with that. Truly, I was at the point where Dr. Chang could have left the oil in forever. Since everything was fine, why fix something that wasn't broken?

That was just a thought; I knew we couldn't do that. While the oil kept everything in place now, it could do harm if it remained in my eye for too long.

Dr. Chang said, "I think it would be safe for me to see you in about a month."

Another small victory. The weekly visits that had been a staple in my schedule were going away, and once again, Dr. Chang gave me a small glimpse into his personality. He was as happy as I was with this progress. My victory was his as well.

Tina and I left the office that day full of hope and life continued to move forward for us. I still couldn't drive, but Tina and I really did return to our lives. Part of that return to normal was socializing with friends, and I enjoyed every bit of it.

However, it wasn't as easy to get back to normal as I thought it would be. While my life had been on hold with all of my surgeries, life moved on with everyone else. One major sign of that was with a young woman who was like a niece to me.

Jasmine was the daughter of a childhood friend of mine, Racquel. Racquel was like family, one of my "sisters" from 1199, the complex where I'd grown up in Harlem. Back then, we really were raised by a village, and Racquel's mom, Helen, was one of my bonus moms. The way she helped raise me really made us as close as any family.

Jasmine was getting married on Labor Day weekend, in Maryland at the National Harbor. As happy and excited as I was for her, I also felt terrible. I still hadn't been released to drive because of the oil in my eye, and Tina was uncomfortable driving long distances.

The call I had to make to Helen (the woman who was like my mom) to tell her I wouldn't be attending the wedding of her granddaughter was more than a little awkward; it was borderline painful. Helen listened to my explanation, but I could tell by her silence at first that she wasn't going to accept it. "Are you sure there's nothing you can do?"

I just kept repeating how I couldn't drive and Tina's discomfort for driving long distances. It seemed, though, that the more I gave my reasons, the more she pressed. She wasn't aggressive, but I was like her son and this was her granddaughter. This was her granddaughter's wedding. She wanted me to be there.

Still, I told her I probably wouldn't be able to make it.

A few weeks later, Tina and I were able to attend Jasmine's bridal shower in New York. There were so many of our friends there as well—Bill and Malika, who were also closer than just friends. We were all sitting around, just talking and catching up when Bill brought up the wedding.

"So, will you guys be staying the whole weekend in Maryland?" he asked, assuming we were going. It was a natural assumption, of course, for family.

Here was another awkward moment when I had to tell family that I couldn't attend.

"No. Tina and I aren't going to be able to make it."

There was shock all around. "What do you mean?" Bill asked.

Again, I explained the situation and like Helen, Bill wasn't having it. "Bullshit," he said. "Y'all are going. Y'all can just ride down with us."

His words were kind of a relief, but at the same time, they made me feel awkward. The awkward part came from my own feeling of inadequacy and had nothing to do with Bill's offer, they were like family, too. This was all about feeling like I couldn't hold my own.

While I could tell that Tina felt the same relief, she had none of the awkwardness. She was filled with excitement; now, we had a way to go to the wedding. Then my wife noticed my reaction and like the wonderful wife that she was, she didn't leave me out there alone. She said, "Okay, well, we'll see," not committing to anything because just by looking at me, she knew I wasn't comfortable with the idea of riding with Bill and Malika.

Tina's words only made Bill press some more. "Nah, come on. Either y'all can ride with us or we can drive down together in our own cars; either way, you'll be fine."

The more he pressed, the worse I felt. I didn't want to be a burden on anyone, and that's what I was feeling. Now, of course, Bill nor anyone else was making me feel this way; this was all my own ego. Finally, I was able to change the subject.

For the next couple of days, Tina and I wrestled with the thought of what we were going to do, asking ourselves how it would look if we weren't there…this was a once-in-a-lifetime occasion…how would the family feel? We didn't have much time to make a decision; the wedding was in a couple of weeks.

Helen called so excited because Bill had told her we were riding with him and Malika. In her mind, it was all settled. Her excitement made me realize I had to put aside my feelings for family. Too many people were counting on us being there. We had to go.

However, I came up with what I called a compromise. We wouldn't drive down; Tina and I would take Amtrak and then we'd ride back with Bill and Malika.

All I can say about this experience is that I'm so glad Helen and Bill pushed because the wedding was something I would have been sorry to miss. So many of my "family" and friends were there, and it was wonderful for us to be celebrating together, surrounded by people who meant so much to me.

The reception was held at The Sunset Room right on the water, and it was a beautiful sight. I even found myself getting a little emotional at the reception, thinking I could have missed all of this because of my crazy thinking.

The celebration continued even after the wedding. The area where we stayed had a bit of a Greenwich Village feel, so we hung out, walking the streets, checking out the stores, and just enjoying ourselves with our friends and family.

The celebration didn't end in Maryland. The ride back with Bill and Malika was just as much fun. We had great conversation, lots of laughs, and stopped off in Philly to see Malika's mom. It was an amazing opportunity to share intimate moments with our extended family.

While we were traveling home, Bill told us he was having a birthday party a few weeks later. After the time I'd had that weekend, I couldn't wait. It would be another gathering of friends and family, this time in New York, up in Harlem. There would be even more people there for me to connect and reconnect with.

Based on the way this weekend had gone, Bill's party couldn't get here fast enough for me.

As time moved on, I was pleased with the way my eye was healing. Since I wasn't seeing Dr. Freilich anymore and seeing Dr. Chang just once a month, I monitored my vision myself. Whenever Tina and I were in the car, I still gaged my vision by the license plates on the cars in front of me. If I could see the letters and the numbers, then all was well.

Still, as the weeks passed, I was happy about my upcoming appointment with Dr. Chang because when he said things were fine, then everything was definitely fine.

As we prepared to leave home for Dr. Chang's office, I was excited, thinking about how well I'd been doing. But once we got into the car, I was a bit pensive. I hadn't had any issues with my eye; I guess it was just natural for me to be a little concerned because I didn't know what Dr. Chang would say or what he would find.

While Tina drove, I, once again, meditated and visualized exactly what I wanted Dr. Chang to say. I imagined my celebration after he told me what I wanted to hear.

It had been a month since we'd been to Dr. Chang's office, so it was good to see all the people who had supported us before. The first person we saw was the garage attendant, Papi, and he grinned widely. In his broken English, he let me know how happy he was to see us and I returned the greeting with my own broken Spanish.

Then, the quietness set in again as Tina and I walked the half block to the hospital. All of our friends (at least that's how I'd come to think of them), greeted us the way they always did. Since I hadn't been here in a while, I knew the staff had figured out I was doing well.

However, as much as I tried to control my thoughts, the anxiety always returned while I sat in Dr. Chang's waiting room, and even when I was taken to the back for the preliminary examination.

When Dr. Chang came into the room, he was the most relaxed I'd ever seen him, and at that moment, I thought back to the very beginning when we first met and he was all business. However, in the space of these months, the doctor and I had been through so much together. He was much more comfortable, and so was I.

After we chatted a bit about how everything was going, Dr. Chang began his examination. I held my breath, but after just a few minutes, he said, "Steve, I have to say, everything looks good."

I exhaled.

"So, how are you feeling? Is everything good with you?"

"Yeah, I don't have anything to complain about." Then I remembered something that had happened to me a couple of times. "There are times, though, only at night, when I get a bit of glare from the traffic lights and it makes my vision cloudy."

He nodded. "That's normal. It's the oil. How long ago did we put in the oil?"

"It was in July," I told him.

He nodded. "Okay, let's see what it looks like in November and maybe we'll start talking about taking it out then."

November? That was two months away. Not needing to see me again for two months was more affirmation that everything was going well. That was my barometer.

Dr. Chang went on to explain that he still didn't want me driving, and he had not yet released me to go to the gym. "No heavy lifting," he also warned.

I understood. He didn't want anything that would put pressure on my eye. Of course, I was willing to follow all of his instructions, but I did have one question.

"You know, Dr. Chang, since everything is going so well, are you sure we have to take the oil out?"

Dr. Chang had already explained how the oil worked, but with everything going so well, I just didn't want to risk another surgery. I didn't want to do anything to mess with my eye.

Dr. Chang smiled, and as patiently as he'd done the first time, he explained the importance of taking the oil out after it had done what we needed it to do. I nodded. If there was anything I knew, it was that Dr. Chang knew what he was doing.

As we stood to leave, I thanked Dr. Chang sincerely as I did every chance I had. I was overwhelmed with gratitude for this man. "I owe all of this to you."

"We did this together, Steve. We just had to get it right."

I walked out of his office ready to take on the next two months. And thinking what I always did when I left Dr. Chang—that he really was a very good man.

169

CHAPTER 27

From the moment Bill told Tina and me about his party, I'd been looking forward to it. Bill was a party promoter, so we all knew it was going to be a fantastic event, made even better because Bill was going to surprise Malika by proposing to her.

The party was held in a bar/lounge and as I said, I'd been excited...until I stepped inside. This was going to be a challenge. Inside the lounge, it was very dark, although that wasn't the only problem. The flashing lights presented me with the most challenges. There was already so much going on in my eye, and now, these lights were not only flashing but were constantly moving, which caused them to reflect off the oil in my eye.

It was continuous and blinding; I couldn't even see people who were standing right in front of me because of the reflections and the glare. My vision was so distorted it became embarrassing when I passed people and I heard, "Hey, Steve, you just gonna walk right past me?"

I began to have the one feeling that I always feared—I felt handicapped because Tina had to start telling me, "Steven, that's so-and-so over there," or "So-and-so is coming over to us now."

Every negative feeling I'd ever had about my situation rose within me. I felt inadequate, I felt like a burden to Tina, and that was when I realized I had only one choice—I had to leave.

Of course, Tina asked no questions when I told her I was ready to go. She understood because she had one goal and that was to take care of me. But the ride home was a bit depressing; what happened in that club was completely unexpected. After Jasmine's wedding in Maryland, I thought I could conquer anything.

I was in a place where I hadn't been in a while—a low point that made me very aware of my situation. After everything I'd been through, after all the work I'd put in, I couldn't even hang out with my friends at a nightclub. It felt kind of like a—don't get too big for your britches—reminder.

My sadness wasn't just about me. Tina had been stuck in the house with me and now, I'd ruined this night for her, too. Of course, she didn't feel that way, but these were my thoughts.

I knew this wasn't how it would always be. This was just an effect of the oil. Tonight, though, felt as if this would be my forever life.

It was clear that I wasn't ready for prime time. For the next few months, Tina, my protector, made sure when we did venture out, we stayed a little closer to home, especially at night.

CHAPTER 28

The weeks moved on and day by day, even after the nightclub fiasco, I was feeling more like myself. The holidays were coming up and this was another time when I couldn't have been more excited. After what I'd been through, I was looking forward to the holiday celebrations and this festive time.

It was especially exciting because this would be the first family gathering Tina would share with her brother.

Tina and I loved to host Thanksgiving, but like all the past years, I was the one who, as we prepared for the celebration of the holiday, mumbled and grumbled my way through. It took a lot to clean the house, to buy the food, and then to cook. But in the end, we'd all sit down, four generations, with me as the patriarch. I couldn't wait to give thanks for everything, especially this past year, in front of the people I loved.

The day turned out to be exactly the way I imagined. We welcomed about twenty-five people that included our daughters and son, Tina's brother, and our friends...oh, and of course, Parker. The day would not have been complete without my granddaughter.

Our apartment was filled with kids running around shouting, adults were sitting and laughing, the television screen was filled with football games, while music played in the background. It was a complete chaotic joy.

When we were finally ready to eat, most of us sat at a festively decorated long table that consisted of two smaller tables pushed together, as well as some who were sitting at our regular dining table. We had the tradition, like most families, of having everyone share what they were thankful for.

I started it off, just to break the ice and set the tone.

"First, Tina and I want to welcome everyone to our home and I want to thank you for joining us for this wonderful holiday. Each of you mean so much to us and we are grateful to have you in our lives. I really want to welcome you, Andre," I said to Tina's brother before I continued.

"I have so much to be grateful for this year because just a few short months ago, it really was touch and go with my eyesight. It's true, we don't appreciate things until there's a chance they will be taken away. So I'm grateful because when I say it's really good to see you, I mean… it's really good to see you."

Even though it was an emotional moment, everyone laughed. We then went around the table. Even the children had a chance to share their gratitude.

The last to speak was Mama D, my friend Franklin's mother. It was appropriate that she be last because she was the elder of the group. She had listened to everyone's statements, so when she spoke, she addressed each of us and what we'd given thanks for.

"This is what life is about," she said to all of us. "We must remember what is important—and that is family and love." She went on to thank Tina and me. "The two of you are really special; you have a special kind of love, don't ever let that fire burn out. The two of you are an example to so many. Look at the generations you've brought together."

Her words were beautiful and touching.

Just hearing everyone speak about their gratitude made all the house cleaning, the numerous trips to the grocery store, and the hours preparing the food worthwhile.

Finally, we said grace, and the apartment filled with the sound of friendly chatter as we all enjoyed the Thanksgiving feast. Hours later, when the last guest walked out of our home close to midnight, Tina and I looked at each other, shared a kiss and a high five. We then sat on the sofa to just chill and reflect on the day, remembering the special moments.

"But we're not doing it again," I said.

Tina just laughed. This was our ongoing joke. I complained and complained…and looked forward to us hosting Thanksgiving every year. Although I had so many Thanksgivings to remember fondly, this one, I knew, would always be one of the best.

Thanksgiving wasn't the only highlight for November. The following Thursday was the first time I would see Dr. Chang in two months. It was interesting; everything was going so well in my life. It was almost like my medical appointments were a thing of the past.

On the morning of my appointment, I couldn't believe that I woke up to old thoughts. Could something go wrong today? Even though two months had passed, I had to go right back to my ritual to control my thoughts: I focused, meditated, and visualized. I centered myself as Tina drove me up to Columbia Presbyterian. I had a great moment of reprieve when I saw Papi in the parking garage.

"There you go," Tina said, as my friend and I greeted each other.

The greetings continued throughout the hospital. Everyone was so glad to see us and even happier to know I was doing well and, according to Dr. Chang, I was doing really well. The appointment was quick and very lighthearted.

"Everything is looking good, Steve," Dr. Chang said after my examination. "I'll see you in two months."

It was clear now that I was truly on my way to complete healing. All that was left was the final surgery to remove the oil and this journey would be over.

Then one morning, a few months after I'd seen Dr. Chang, I was sitting at my desk at work and suddenly, something didn't seem right in my eye. The reflection was different and there was more waviness in the oil.

I wasn't sure if it was the way the oil had settled in my eye or what, but this was different than the flashing lights and floaters I was used to. For a while, I tried to sit back and wait. Was this just my mind playing tricks? The challenge was, I couldn't talk myself down. I was already in that zone. Once I'd told myself something was wrong, I was all the way there.

For a while, I sat at my desk, thinking, This can't be happening. Not now. Not when I was so close to the end.

I tried to put this out of my mind and just get back to work. It was hard for me to function and focus. Even though I didn't say anything about what was going on to anyone, everybody could see I was distracted. People would speak to me and I barely heard what was being said. I just couldn't concentrate.

A little after noon, I couldn't take it anymore. I called Dr. Chang's office and was told to come in right away. Dr. Chang was across town that day so I wouldn't have to go up to Columbia Presbyterian, which was good. His 53rd Street office was much closer.

Before I left work, I decided to call Tina. I certainly didn't want to worry her, but if she called the office and I wasn't there, that was exactly what she'd do.

When she picked up the phone, I said, "Listen, babe. I'm heading to Dr. Chang. Something seems off."

She was silent, as if she was trying to absorb my words. But even though I knew she was shocked, she went right into positive mode.

"It's going to be fine," she said. "Just call me when you're done."

On the entire trip across town, I focused, meditated, then visualized the way I wanted this to end.

Inside Dr. Chang's office, after I'd checked in, one of Dr. Chang's assistants gave me an examination and the first thing she wanted to do was test my vision.

As I looked at the vision chart, I prayed: God, I can't do this again.

The assistant said, "Okay, go ahead and start reading."

I began and all the lines were clear. When I got to the 20/40 line, I stopped.

"Keep going," the assistant said. When I remained quiet, she repeated, "Keep going."

So, I did. I read four out of the five letters, but you only need to read three to have that vision. I had 20/30—for the first time ever. I'd come to Dr. Chang's office to find out what was wrong, and my vision was better than it had ever been.

This was huge. I had good vision test scores before…20/50 and even 20/40. But 20/30 was as close as I could get without having perfect vision.

"It seems like everything is okay," the assistant said. "Let me get Dr. Chang."

I was relieved, but now, I was also a little embarrassed. I'd had all of these hours of mental hysteria for nothing. Now I felt like I was wasting the doctor's time. I explained it all to Dr. Chang when he came into the examination room.

"Well, let me take a look at your eye, anyway." It didn't take long for Dr. Chang to have me sitting up again. "Things look great."

"You don't know how good it is to hear that."

Dr. Chang said, "I don't know what was going on with you earlier. It could have just been a shift in the oil. And you know when that happens, it changes the refractions."

I nodded; I knew this, but I had allowed my thoughts to get away from me.

He said, "How long has it been since your surgery?"

This had become like a little shtick between us. At every appointment, he asked that question.

"It was July," I told him again.

"Okay, well, we really need to start thinking about taking the oil out. I think we'll look at it toward May or June."

"Okay," I said. This was where I should have really been excited. Not only was there nothing wrong with my eye, but taking the oil out would be the end.

However, once again I was battling old thoughts, wondering if we should just leave the oil right where it was. Was my retina stable enough for the oil to be removed? Did I want to take that chance?

I did what I could to push those thoughts aside. If there was anything positive about the anxiety I'd had over these months, it was that I'd learned to control my thoughts, to channel negative energy, to dig deep, and really rely on my faith. I learned to build up resistance to negativity with all kinds of techniques.

So I replaced the negative thoughts with new ones. I celebrated the fact that I'd faced blindness and beat it. I was prepared for anything I had to face in the future...including the final surgery.

CHAPTER 29

One month later, during my appointment with Dr. Chang, he asked me that question again. "So, how long has it been since your surgery? Since we put in the oil?"

I glanced at the residents who were with him and smiled. They had heard him ask this question a couple of dozen times, too.

When I told him it was in July, he said, "So, it's coming up on a year. I think we're ready to take it out." He paused for a moment. "I'll be back in June. Let's schedule it for then so I can monitor you afterward."

I agreed to the date, thankful that it gave me a little time to get used to the idea of another operation. It also gave me and Tina the opportunity to travel to Mexico. We affectionately called that trip the Mexican Takeover.

Bill and Malika were getting married, and like every other event Bill planned, we knew this was going to be a fabulous weekend. They'd invited about one hundred friends and family members to celebrate their wedding for five days at a fabulous resort. While we were there, I didn't have a single thought about my upcoming surgery. Between the parties, the food, and the fun, there wasn't time for me to do anything except live in those moments.

There were a few times when it was a bit challenging because the resort, at night, had a club atmosphere with the flashing lights. But it wasn't as crazy as the club in Harlem. So I was able to relax and just enjoy myself.

Like all good things, the vacation came to an end and when we returned to New York, it was time for me to prepare for the surgery that would take place on Tuesday, June 19.

The first thing I had to do was get cleared by my primary care doctor, just like all the other times. Then, I had to fill out all the forms from Dr. Chang's office as well, so I was covered on all fronts.

Once that was all in place, I had to let Alex know I was going to be out of work. "It'll be for a week or two," I told Alex, and then I added, "Definitely just a week or two this time."

I'd done so well since I'd returned to work, I knew he believed me; he wasn't concerned.

Of all the surgeries I'd had during this process, I was most relaxed about this one. Yes, I was still a bit anxious, but this time Dr. Chang wasn't going in to repair something. This was all about bringing this part of my journey to a close.

I kept the same rituals in place, though, speaking to Cousin Stephanie and Evangelist Jessup the night before as they prayed over me, and I spoke to Smitty and my brother. My goal was to center myself using all the techniques that had worked for me through this last year.

This was definitely a different feel, though, because the night before this surgery, I was filled with peace.

The routine for this surgery was the same as the ones before. I was in early for my patient intake and greeted again by the hospital staff as if I were an old friend. The medical team got me prepped and ready for surgery, washing my face, applying eye drops to numb the nerves, taking my blood pressure, having me change into a surgical gown and socks, and asking all the intake questions, making sure I hadn't eaten since midnight. I'd been here so much it almost felt as if I could have done the intake myself.

Once my in-room preparation was complete, I kissed Tina, and they rolled me up to the operating room. While I wouldn't be fully unconscious for the surgery, I was given a mild sedative before Dr. Chang came in.

"Okay, Steve," Dr. Chang began. "We're going to do this."

Dr. Chang began the surgery, and then I heard him turn over the operation to one of his residents. That was surprising, but the sedative kept me calm. Plus, I wasn't really concerned; Dr. Chang was still there. It was a quick procedure, less than an hour and I was done.

"You're all set, Steve," Dr. Chang said as they began to patch up my eye.

I was taken back to the room and even though I hadn't been given anesthesia, I had to wait there for a while, just enough time for the sedative to wear off a bit.

A nurse came into the room and took me through all the post-op questions. "Are you okay?"

"Yes," I told her.

"No nausea or anything?"

"No, I feel fine."

Just when she finished, the hospital attendant appeared with the apple juice and graham crackers.

As if all of this was timed, Dr. Chang stopped by at that moment.

"Everything went well, Steve. We got the oil out and your retina looks great."

I breathed. So relieved.

"I want to see you tomorrow," he said.

"Okay," I told him.

"Keep the patch on for tonight," he told me. "You'll be able to take it off tomorrow."

Once he left the room, the nurse gave me the same eye drops that I'd have to have three times a day. Once I dressed and finally settled in the wheelchair to be rolled out of the hospital, it hit me—I wouldn't be coming back here.

On the way out, I thanked everyone for the professional care they'd always given to me. Tina left me in the hospital room lobby under the watchful eye of the security guard while she went to get the car. When she returned, as careful as she always was, my wife held my arm and led me to the car, directing me step-by-step.

For the first time, I had a list of great things about this ride home from the hospital. First, I didn't have to keep my head down. Next, the entire ride was relaxing. Tina and I chatted easily, both of us realizing that we'd come to the end.

When I got home I rested, which was what I always did since we had the earliest appointment. Today, I think my exhaustion was more mental than physical; I needed to rest my mind, not from this surgery, but from all the thoughts and emotions I'd carried throughout this journey.

When I woke up, I called Smitty and my brother. I told them the surgery had gone well; the oil was out and these kinds of calls had come to an end. Of course, we'd still talk all the time, but we'd chat about other things now. This part was over and I saw nothing but good times in my future.

CHAPTER 30

For too many hours throughout the night, I tossed and turned until I couldn't do it anymore. It was about five in the morning when I woke up and carefully felt my way into the bathroom. Turning on the light, I took a breath as I looked in the mirror. Questions overwhelmed me: When I removed this patch, what would my vision be like without the oil? How much better would it be without the refractions?

I inhaled deeply before I removed the patch.

Right away I could tell there was definitely a difference, but I was disappointed. My vision wasn't as clear as it had been. In fact, there were little circles in my eye. They weren't like the long squiggly floaters that I was used to, but whenever I shifted my eye, I saw these bubbles with dark rings around them. There weren't a lot of them; just enough to be noticeable, just enough to make me concerned.

Now, like I said, I always had a lot going on in my eye, but this was new and it was this newness that caused all of my anxiety to rush back.

I could still see well enough, but this had certainly knocked a bit of wind out of my sail.

When Tina awakened, the first thing she asked was, "How's your sight without the patch?"

I heard the excited anticipation in her voice and all I said was, "Great, everything's fine."

There was no way I wanted to tell her, no way I wanted her to share in my disappointment, at least not yet. We prepared for our post-surgery appointment the way we always did. When we got into the car, I was quiet, the way I always was, so Tina didn't really notice. She probably thought I was just focusing, but for the entire ride to Dr. Chang's Midtown office, all I could do was to wonder if this was a setback.

I wouldn't be able to keep what was going on from Tina for very long. Once we arrived at Dr. Chang's office for my appointment and the assistant had me take the vision test, it was clear that my vision wasn't what it had been. Now it was 20/50.

I could see that at first Tina was confused because of what I'd told her this morning when she asked. I knew she was wondering what happened to the 20/30 vision. Then, I saw it in her eyes; her disappointment matched mine.

Both of us perked up a bit when Dr. Chang entered and once again reiterated that the surgery had gone well. After he examined my eye, he said, "Everything looks good, Steve."

His words helped to calm me a little. "I'm glad to hear that because I was a little concerned. I have these little circles with dark outlines in my eyes. I've never had this before."

He nodded, as if he knew exactly what I was talking about. "That's just little oil droplets we couldn't get out. It's impossible to get every drop of oil out of your eye, but we remove as much as we can."

"Oh," I said, surprised. I'd never thought of that. "So will it stay this way?"

"No, it will settle down. It won't ever go away completely, but it'll become less noticeable. And you probably also still have some inflammation from the surgery. I'm going to adjust your prescription, so your sight will improve over time."

Now, I was fine and for the next couple of weeks, I continued going to post-op appointments. Dr. Chang wasn't concerned; he just wanted to make sure it was all on track and to see if my prescription ever needed to be adjusted. He had to adjust my prescription once, but at every appointment, Dr. Chang said the same thing: "Everything looks good, Steve."

With the oil out, my life had pretty much returned to what it was before my first surgery. It was summer, so after work and on the weekends, Tina and I took advantage of that, hanging out, just the two of us, or with friends. It was so good to get out and enjoy this time of the year since we'd spent most of the last summer not being able to do anything. We had a lot of time to make up.

Every couple of weeks I saw Dr. Chang, and by now it felt like he was more than my doctor. We were very familiar with each other, joking all the time. However, the best parts of every appointment were the way it started with, "How are you doing, Steve?" and ended with, "Everything looks good."

When I received my final prescription, I wanted to make sure I had a nice pair of glasses. Getting glasses may seem like such a simple task, but the challenge with my glasses was that I had a special prescription for ultra-thin lenses. These lenses were not only specialized but expensive. They'd been developed so someone like me wouldn't have to walk around with Coke-bottle thick glasses.

I had a close friend, Harold, who I'd known for years. Harold, who sold designer frames, was a blessing, not only because he could meet me at my home or my office, but he could get me any kind of glasses—regular, sunglasses, any kind of tint I wanted with my prescription—at deeply discounted prices. My prescription at any of the national chains would have cost hundreds of dollars, but Harold was always able to work out an attractive deal that gave me high quality at rock-bottom prices.

So, life moved along...until August 2. At that appointment, Dr. Chang examined my eye the way he always did, and at the end, he told me the same thing. "Everything looks good." Then, he added words I'd been waiting to hear for more than a year. "Steve, I think we finally got you out of the woods."

There were very few times when I became emotional during this process, but hearing those words made me as emotional as I'd ever been. Dr. Chang was telling me this was over. This was officially over. I had made it all the way to the other side.

As I sat there for a few moments, my life over the last year flashed through my mind like movie scenes: Being on an operating table for the first surgery and then having to hold my head down. The disappointment when Dr. Chang had to go back in and my crying out to God. I remembered the Fourth of July picnic, the fiasco at the nightclub, and the joy of Jasmine's wedding. I recalled how my life started to come back together when I returned to work, even the catastrophe of that Monday morning, my first day back.

It had been a roller coaster of a year, with peaks and valleys, highs and lows, victories and setbacks. I'd experienced joy and anger, frustration and paranoia, and most of all, anxiety. I'd been exhausted physically, mentally, and emotionally, although I had stayed steady spiritually.

That was the best part of this journey, besides having my eyesight. I had been gifted with a greater awareness of God. I realized that God wasn't going to put me through something that He wasn't going to give me everything I needed to pull through. On those days when I felt like my eye was being held together by duct tape, I had (and still have) the best wife in the world, the best doctor in the world, and a support team of people who had prayed, listened, and just kept me sane. With all that God had given to me, I persevered, never gave up, never thought of quitting.

It was because I hadn't given up, and no one had given up on me, that I was able to celebrate now. I felt jubilant and what I realized, even more, was that I had a story to tell. After all that God had done for me, I couldn't keep this test, nor this testimony, to myself. What I'd gone through wasn't for me alone, and I was going to find some way to share this.

After I poured out all of my emotion and gratitude to Dr. Chang, I felt compelled to say, "Dr. Chang, if you know of any place where I can speak and help people who may be going through something like this, let me know. I want to help. I want to give back."

Dr. Chang nodded. "I don't know of any place, but from time to time I do have people who have serious conditions like yours. If you want, I can give them your number if they ever need anyone to talk to."

"Yes," I nodded, "I'd love to do that. Please don't hesitate to pass on my number to anyone who needs it."

After we shook hands, he said goodbye to Tina, and we walked out of his office feeling as if a thousand-pound weight had been lifted from our shoulders. When I turned to Tina, all the emotions I experienced were on her face, too. My biggest cheerleader was filled with all the happiness that I felt. A Godly pride bubbled up inside of me. I'd made it through, not just for myself, but for my wife and my family, too. We had made it together.

It was in the first part of September when I got a call from the resident who'd worked with Dr. Chang during my last surgery. I was surprised to hear from him. At first, the conversation was really casual. He asked how I was doing and how I'd been feeling, leaving me puzzled as to why he was calling.

Finally, he said, "Well, I wanted to let you know that Dr. Chang has a patient who has a situation that is similar to yours..."

Then, I remembered my offer to Dr. Chang.

The doctor went on to explain that their patient had no sight in one eye and his surgery was very risky. "I remember you telling Dr. Chang if we ever had anybody who was facing something like this, you would speak to them."

"Oh, yes," I said right away. "Give him my number, please."

The doctor thanked me and told me to expect a call. Two days later, I received a call from a number I didn't recognize. I didn't answer, but I checked my voicemail messages.

"Hello, Steve. My name is Jonathan. Dr. Chang told me to call you…"

I called Jonathan right back. After we introduced ourselves, I asked him what was going on. He was timid at the start, telling me a little about his situation. I understood his hesitation. He didn't know me, didn't know what to expect from me, and he was obviously going through his own emotions with his situation. I wanted him to feel as comfortable as possible from the gate. But there was something I wanted him to know from the beginning—and that was about Dr. Chang.

"The first thing you have to know is that you're in the best hands possible. The best hands in the world, literally. You've got to know that."

That helped Jonathan open up a bit, but rather than just talking about his situation, I wanted him to feel more comfortable with me. We started talking about our families and the things we liked to do. We talked about sports. He was a big fantasy football player, something I'd never done but was very interested in hearing about as I was a big football fan myself.

By the time we began talking about our histories, we had already started bonding. I figured the best way to make Jonathan comfortable with Dr. Chang was to tell him a bit about my situation.

"I was seven when I had my first operation," I told him. "And I've had thirteen more surgeries since then."

Jonathan reacted the way everyone did to that fact. "Wow!" he said.

"So, I know a little bit about what you're going through." I went on to tell him everything that I'd been through, up to my operation with Dr. Chang. "Literally, he saved the quality of my life. I'm really grateful to him."

Jonathan went on to tell me about his situation. He had 20/400 vision in one eye. He wondered if having the surgery was even worth it, given the condition of his eye. I told him that saving his eye was worth it. With the way technology was progressing, one day there might be a way to have his eyesight completely restored, so taking the chance now was the right thing to do.

As we talked, I realized that in so many ways, while it seemed like we'd grown up and lived on opposite ends of the world, we had so much in common.

"Wow," I said after he told me all that he'd been through.

Talking about our situations bonded us further. Jonathan said, "I never thought I'd meet someone who could identify with what I was going through."

"I know what you mean," I said. "I had a lot of support from my wife, my brother, my family, and my friends, but there's nothing like talking this through with someone who's been through a similar situation. That's why I wanted to talk to you."

"Well, I'm glad your situation worked out for you, but I'm just not sure," Jonathan said. He went on to explain the type of surgery he would need, which was much more complex than mine. Jonathan needed two procedures at one time. Dr. Chang would perform the one that would repair his retina, and then another doctor would have to put a tube into his eye to relieve the pressure.

It was overwhelming to Jonathan because he didn't feel like he had a lot of options. "If I have the surgery and it doesn't work, what will happen? But if I don't do anything, it will only get worse."

"I understand how you feel because I felt the same way," I told him. "I had the same questions, the same doubts, and I did feel kind of trapped. But again, you've got to know, and this is no exaggeration, you're dealing with the best guy in the world for your situation. And think about it, what are the odds that you get the doctor who's the top in the world? That has to mean something."

We stayed on the phone for an hour. As Jonathan shared all his concerns, I talked through each point with him. We bonded, we cried, and by the time we finished the call for the night, Jonathan was like my brother from another mother.

"I'm so grateful you spent this time with me," he said. "But I'm still not sure what I'm going to do."

I understood. I didn't make my decision right away either. This was tough. Whichever decision he made was going to be life-changing.

"That's fine," I said. "This is one of the most important decisions you'll ever make. You should take your time. But just know that I'm going to be here, so any questions you have, any time you want to talk, you have my number."

When we finally hung up, I was filled with a feeling that I knew I would never forget. I think it came from the fact that when someone like me grows up with such a unique situation, you feel like you're the only one on the planet who was going through it. Even though family and friends tried, no one could ever fully relate to or understand all the emotions of a journey such as mine.

Speaking to Jonathan felt almost like a sign from God. To be speaking to someone so similar to me was definitely divinely ordered.

I couldn't wait to share this with Tina. When I called her, it all spilled out of me—what Jonathan and I had shared, how we had bonded, and how much I really wanted to help him.

Tina said, "That's wonderful. I'm so happy you're getting to do this."

I smiled. I was really happy about it, too.

CHAPTER 31

J onathan and I talked a few more times. Whenever he
called me, the call began tentatively. "I hate to bother
you," he would always say, even though I tried to assure
him it was never a bother, but my pleasure to help if I could.

"Listen, man, call me anytime. I don't care what kind of
questions you have, just call me."

He was grateful for my words, but his uncertainty
remained. Basically, he kept asking himself the same question:
Should I do this or should I leave it alone? After the third call,
I suggested we meet for dinner, and he agreed.

In the beginning, I wanted to be a sounding board for
Jonathan as he worked it out in his mind. However, I also
wanted to convince him to do the operation, because it would
only get worse if he did nothing...and he had Dr. Chang on
his side.

We decided to meet at Mr. Broadway's in Midtown. I
arrived a few minutes before he did. As I waited in front of
the restaurant, Jonathan showed up, called out my name, and
walked up to me. He held out his hand to shake mine, but I

pulled him into an embrace. I'm sure he felt a little awkward, but it didn't matter; we had bonded as brothers.

Inside the restaurant, we chatted like old friends as we talked about our families. I told him more about Tina and he shared about his girlfriend and his parents, who had passed away. We soon got to our favorite subject: sports, specifically football.

By the time our meals came, we finally turned our discussion to his pending surgery. I was a bit surprised at his continued hesitation, knowing what the alternative was, but I kept telling him I understood. There were a lot of risks with the surgery. This was his eye, his life—he was the only one who would live with his decision.

While the risks were clear, I wanted to help Jonathan see the rewards. Once again, I reiterated all I'd told him about Dr. Chang.

"If you do nothing, it will get worse. The only chance you have is to put this in Dr. Chang's hands. That's the only way this will improve for you."

By the end of the dinner, Jonathan said, "Steve, I'm going to do it."

I was so happy with his decision. "You know what? I'm going to be there with you. I'm going to be there at the hospital," I told him.

He shook his head. "I can't allow you to do that."

"Well, you can't stop me. I'm going to be there. I want to be there to support you."

We went back and forth discussing this for a few minutes, but I wasn't going to budge. The moment those words came out of my mouth, I knew I was supposed to do it.

"Wow," was what Jonathan finally said when he realized he wasn't going to change my mind.

When he blinked back tears, again, I understood. My support meant a lot because he didn't have many who would be able to support him. That didn't matter, though. I would be there.

From that point on I became like the big brother, filling Jonathan in on what it was going to be like and all of the things he'd have to do.

"Keeping your head down is going to be the hardest part. Who's going to help you afterward?" I asked. "Because you won't be able to be out there on your own."

"I have a couple of friends on the Upper West Side. I'll be staying with them until I'm able to go back to my place." He paused and added, "I don't know how to thank you."

"You already have." I tried to explain to Jonathan how this was a blessing for me. The two of us couldn't have been any more different, something we really discovered the one time we discussed politics. We were far apart when it came to those beliefs, and after a very spirited conversation, we retreated to our corners and knew that wasn't a discussion we'd ever revisit.

Despite that, Jonathan and I were two men who discovered that though I was Black and he was White, though I was spiritual and he was religious, though I was this big six-foot-two guy and he was of medium height, we had more similarities than differences. It was because of those similarities that I was going to do everything I could for Jonathan.

—◦◦◉◦—

The date of his surgery had already been set, but Jonathan had waited until the last minute to make his decision. So once he said yes, everything was full speed ahead. Jonathan and I talked on the phone at least three more times before the day of his surgery, and it was a good thing because I almost think if he didn't have me to share everything with, he may have talked himself out of it.

"Steve, I'm still questioning whether I'm making the right decision," he said more than once. "You know, what if it doesn't work?"

It wasn't hard for me to be patient with Jonathan. He didn't have the support system I had before each of my surgeries. He didn't have a Tina at home or a Cousin Stephanie and Evangelist Jessup a phone call away. He didn't have a brother, Michael, or a friend like Smitty who he could vent to at any hour of the day.

I wanted to be that support for him and kept reminding him of what was most important. "Just remember, you have Dr. Chang. He will take care of you." That was my mantra because I knew that was the truth.

The night before the surgery, I offered to take Jonathan to the hospital the next morning, but he told me his friend was going to drop him off. So, I arranged to meet him there and drive him home. Earlier in the week, I'd told Natalie and Alex that I was going to be out for the day.

"I'll be at the hospital. I'm going to support a guy who's going through a similar eye surgery."

Their reactions were the same. Both of them had a look of shock that was mixed with admiration.

"I'm impressed that you're going to do that," Natalie said. "Good for you."

I wasn't doing this to impress anyone. This was all about helping Jonathan get through it.

When I arrived at the hospital the next morning, I experienced something that surprised me. As I walked inside, I had a bit of anxiety. Of course, when I saw the same people, like Papi (who had never seen me driving) and the security guard, I was happy to see them. They were happy to see me, too—once I explained that I was there for a friend.

After I made it past the staff, though, I once again felt like I was the criminal returning to the scene of the crime. Even when I met Jonathan in his room and he introduced me to his friend, I had butterflies as all the memories of me being in that bed where Jonathan was now, rushed back.

As the nurses prepped him, I zoned out a bit, imagining myself in that bed with the nurse next to me and those rubber-soled socks on my feet.

I had a bit of a break from my nervousness as the nurses greeted me, treating me as if I were family. That helped to relax me a bit and return my focus to Jonathan. I began going through a checklist with him:

"Did you wash your face with that special soap?"

"Did you put all your stuff away?"

"Did they start putting drops in your eyes?"

He answered yes to everything and then thanked me again.

When the attendant came to take Jonathan into surgery, I assured him, once again, all that he already knew—that he was in the right hands and that I would be waiting for him when he came back down.

After they rolled Jonathan out of the room, I had to do something I'd never done…I had to find the waiting room. I knew there was one; that's where Tina waited for me. It was another surreal moment when I had to find that room for myself.

When I entered the room that was just down the hall, only three people were sitting in the chairs that were lined up against the wall. Good Morning America was playing on a mounted television.

I greeted everyone with a hearty, "Good morning," before I sat down.

"What are you so chipper about?" one of the guys said. His tone was much lighter than his words, so I knew he was joking.

I said, "I'm chipper because just a year ago, I was the guy being wheeled upstairs. I was the one on the surgery table."

"What do you mean?"

Now the other guy and the woman who sat in the room turned to me. It looked like they all wanted me to explain, so I told them my story. When I finished, the woman said, "That's amazing, and you're amazing for being here for your friend."

After I chatted a little with them, I texted Tina just to give her an update. However, no matter what I tried to do to keep myself occupied, I couldn't shake the out-of-body experience I was feeling.

Jonathan's surgery was going to be much longer than mine since he was having two procedures. I was aware of this, but still, after the second hour, I was getting antsy. I tried to fill the time by doing some work, checking emails, and going onto social media. After a while, I went down to the cafeteria, something else that was a new experience. It was the middle of the day, so I was caught up in the hustle and bustle of the hospital at lunchtime. Doctors and other medical staff were taking quick breaks, mingling and talking. This was another thing that was very much part of my journey, but something I'd never seen. From the waiting room to the cafeteria, this had been Tina's world during all of my surgeries.

I was back in the waiting room when about four hours later, one of the nurses came looking for me. "They just brought Jonathan down," she said. "He's in his room."

For the first time I relaxed, and when I walked out of the waiting room, I felt even better. Dr. Chang and Dr. Liebmann, who both performed Jonathan's surgery, were standing right outside of his room.

"Hey, Steve." Dr. Chang greeted me like a friend. "How's it going? Jonathan told me you were coming here." He nodded. "That's a really nice thing you did for him."

He introduced me to Dr. Liebmann and I thought about how blessed Jonathan was to have two of the top men in their fields operating on him.

Dr. Chang asked how Tina and I were doing in general.

It was good to tell him that I was doing well, but I asked him what I really wanted to know. "How's Jonathan?"

"It went well, but you know how these things go. We'll know in the future."

Once again, he'd given me one of those doctor answers. Nothing could be predicted, nothing could be promised, nothing could be guaranteed.

I said goodbye to the doctors and went into Jonathan's room. He was still groggy, of course, and again, my mind took me back to that place when I was just waking up and wondering what was going to happen now.

At this moment, I was really glad to be here for Jonathan because I knew what he was feeling, I knew his anxiety. With his head down and the patch over his eye, he wouldn't be able to see much, even though he did have sight in his other eye. The world would be so different for the next few weeks.

When he glanced up at me, I said, "Hey, buddy, how's it going?" He nodded a little. "We got through it," I told him.

I stepped aside when the nurses came in to check him and asked him questions that I could recite by heart.

"How are you feeling? No nausea? Are you hungry?"

Jonathan was given the same apple juice and the same graham crackers. It took some time for him to get oriented enough to get dressed and ready to be discharged. But that was fine; I waited for him the way Tina had waited for me. Once the nurses gave him the final instructions and the bags filled with eye drops, I walked with one of the attendants as they wheeled Jonathan downstairs.

He waited with the security guard, as I always did, only now, I was the one to go to the parking garage. That gave me a chance to say goodbye to Papi and thank him once again for everything.

The attendant and I helped Jonathan from the hospital's entrance to the car. Again, it was strange to be the one on the other side, making sure Jonathan was secure before I trotted around to the driver's side. When I got into the car and glanced over at him, I had to take a moment—Jonathan had his head down and a plethora of feelings rushed over me.

Finally, I smiled and turned on the ignition.

The ride to Jonathan's friend's house was filled with light chatter, which made me happy. I knew this was tough for him—his emotions, his concern, the tension in his neck. For the moment, Jonathan wasn't showing any of that. We talked about fantasy football and how excited I was to be joining a league for the first time.

"You'll be a pro like me in no time," he said. All of a sudden, our conversation took a more serious turn. "I don't know how I'll ever be able to repay you for all of this, Steve."

"Oh, you're going to repay me. All you gotta do is help me pick my fantasy football team."

He chuckled, then asked, "Did you speak to Dr. Chang?"

"Yeah, I saw him and Dr. Liebmann when they were coming out of your room."

He nodded but didn't ask what they'd said. "Isn't this crazy? Just a year ago you were up on that operating table and today you're driving me home from the hospital."

That was another emotionally revealing moment that filled me with joy.

All morning I'd been thinking about different parts of my journey, but I hadn't put a timeline to it. It had just been a year. That's it. I knew that, of course, but while I'd been going through it, it seemed so much longer. However, riding in the car with Jonathan, I really got a chance to put this in perspective. In the overall scope of time and how my eye (and therefore the quality of my life) had been saved, a year wasn't anything. I prayed that his words and the realization of what I'd gone through and come through gave Jonathan hope.

Jonathan and I shared one more humorous moment. He told me that when I dropped him off at his friend's home, the nanny would be there to meet him.

When he told me that, I joked with him. "Is the nanny hot?"

"I don't know," he said. "I've never seen her."

We laughed about that for a few moments until I pulled up in front of the house. I said, "She's waiting out there for you."

Jonathan grinned. "Is she hot?"

I didn't answer him, even though he kept asking me. I just helped him out of the car. She came over and introduced herself to both of us.

"Hi, my name is Olga," she said. And that was all she had to say.

I helped Jonathan into the house and then left him in the good care of his friends, reminding him that I was just a phone call away. When I got back into the car, I called Tina and told her the most impactful thing that Jonathan had said to me on this day.

"He's right," I said. "Just a year ago, I was in his position. Just one year."

"Wow," she said, having the same reaction as I did. I could tell she was having the same thoughts—we'd come a long way in a year.

As I drove home, I meditated on the day that I'd had. Now, I understood why I'd had this journey. Everything I'd been through had been worth it for me, for Jonathan, and for anyone else I'd be able to help in the future.

I'd always been a grateful person and had kept my gratitude throughout this time, but I'd never been more thankful than at this moment when I was able to give back to someone who really needed it.

From the time I was seven, I'd had questions about why I had to go through all of this, and now, Jonathan helped me to answer those questions. He'd helped me to understand part of my purpose. God had taken me to the other side and with the blessings that He'd given to me, God wanted me to reach back and pull someone else through.

Right there in my car I made a promise. I was going to do that from now on. I was going to reach back and pay forward every chance I had.

ABOUT THE AUTHOR

A native New Yorker, Steven Anthony King is a public speaker, certified relationship coach, talk show host, co-founder of Complete Chocolate Couples, and the author of It's Really Good to see You. With a corporate background in sales, sales training, and executive sales management that spans over three decades, his purpose is to educate, motivate, and inspire others through sharing the victory of his many life experiences. He lives by three simple words: Purpose, Positivity, and Perseverance. He is a devoted husband, proud father of three, and grandfather of one.

"I give so much because I've been given so much."
– Steven Anthony King

https://www.itsreallygoodtoseeyou.com/

Made in the USA
Middletown, DE
01 June 2021